I WILL MAKE YOU CLICK

JAMES PREECE

WWW.JAMESPREECE.COM

Copyright © 2015 by James Preece

All rights reserved. This book or any portion thereof may not be reproduced or used in any manner whatsoever without the express written permission of the publisher except for the use of brief quotations in a book review.

First Printing, 2015

ISBN-13:

978-1505470277

ISBN-10:

1505470277

Cupid Inc Press

www.jamespreece.com

To Tania and Phoenix

My proudest Dating Guru qualifications

CONTENTS

Introduction 12

Chapter One : Who Do You Want To Meet? 25

    Time to break the Rules – Online Dating Misconceptions 32

    My Huge Dating Tip: The High Street Test: 36

    Are You Ready For Love? Having a Positive Mental Attitude .. 37

    What you have to offer Mr or Miss Right? 39

Chapter Two : Choosing the Right Website 44

    Free Dating or Scams? 46

    The Best Time of Year to Sign up to a Dating Site 49

    Making Payment 50

    Optional Extras and Upgrades - Are they Worth Paying for? ... 50

    How long should you sign up for? 51

    Getting Started 54

Chapter Three : Creating an Irresistible Profile 61

    Choosing a Powerful Username 62

    Your Headline 64

    The Perfect Profile Formula 67

    The Hook 70

    Things you Must Never Say! 71

    Personality Forms and Quizzes 74

Example Profiles 76

Chapter Four : How to Wow them with Gorgeous Photos 84

    The Two Secrets to a Great Photo 85

    What if You Really Don't Want to Add a Photo? 89

    Your Main Photo 90

    How to look your Best 91

    What to Avoid 93

    The Rotation Trick 94

    Ask Friends 95

    Tools of the Trade 96

    Getting the Professionals In 98

Chapter Five : Getting Used to the Site (Upping your Game) 99

    Learn to Use the Filters 100

    Adding to Favourites 100

    When Should you Respond? 101

    Instant Messaging 102

    The Truth about 'Winks" 103

    Who's Online? 105

    The Best Times and Day of the Week to Use a Dating Site ... 106

    Location, Location, Location. How Far Should you Cast your Net? 108

Chapter Six : First Contact and Magical Messages 110

How Men and Women Act Differently on Dating Sites 110

What you Need to Say 112

Time Saving Tip: Learning to Scan 113

How to Handle a Blank Profile 114

Warning! Copy and Pasting – the Lazy Dater's Quickest Route to Failure 115

The Beginning: Get Them to Open Your Email 116

The End - Signing Off 118

How to Guarantee your Profile is Always at the Top of Searches 118

Winning Email Templates 120

Getting Too Many Emails? 123

Second Chances 125

The Games People Play 126

Chapter Seven : How to Get a Date 129

Asking for a Date by Computer 129

Asking for a Date by Phone 130

Sounds Good 132

The First Phone Call 133

Asking the Big Question 135

What to Say if you Can't Get them to Agree to a Date 136

The Joy of Text 137

Sexting 140

How to Prepare for an Amazing Date 143

Chapter Eight : Meeting Up: How to Have the Perfect First Date 146

    Safety First 146

    The Dating Guru Rules 147

    My Good Dating Cheat Sheet 152

    How Men and Women Think Differently when it comes to Dating 154

    How to Flirt 156

    How to Tell if they are Interested 158

    The Friends Zone 159

    How to Spot a Liar 160

    Be on Time 163

    How to Escape a Terrible Date 164

    What You Need to Do Next 167

    The Art of Multi Dating 169

    Dealing with Rejection 170

    The Ghost Date: The Online Dating Phenomena 171

Chapter Nine : The Dark Side of Online Dating: Scammers, Conmen and Catfish 173

    The Fake Profile Scam 173

    The Catfish Scam – Are you Being Baited? 176

    The Nigerian Romance Scam 178

The Russian Romance Scam 182

The Already Taken Scam 184

The Webcam Scam 184

The Reformed Scammer Scam 185

How to Identify if Someone is Genuine................................. 186

What to Do About Them 189

Chapter Ten : How to get Unlimited Dates through Social Media Sites 190

The Basics of Social Media and Getting a Date 191

Fun and Flirting on Facebook 192

Using your Existing Friends and Networks to Help.............. 195

Twitter Tactics 197

LinkedIN to Love 198

Work out what you are Interested in 199

Chapter Eleven : Love at First Swipe – Dating Apps and The Future of Dating 203

A Quick Guide to Tinder 203

How to Avoid Cheats and Timewasters on Dating Apps 209

The Future of Online Dating 211

What will Happen Next? 212

Chapter Twelve : Happily Ever After: (How to Keep it Going) 214

How Soon Should I Commit?.. 214

Are they Really the Right Person for You? 217

Dealing with Jealousy and Trust Issues in a Relationship 218

The Right Time to Delete your Profile 220

Meeting and Getting on with their Friends and Family 222

How to Survive a Long Distance Relationship 224

Don't Give Up 225

Dating Guru's Dating Directory 230

Online Dating Sites 230

Other Useful Sites 233

Launching your Own Dating Site 233

Scammer Databases 234

Reverse Image Checking Sites 234

Personal Dating Coaching 235

Dating Apps 235

About the Author 237

Acknowledgements

This book has taken a long time to write because it's based on so many years of real life online dating experience. In this time I have been fortunate enough to meet so many wonderful people and to have such supportive friends and family.

There are hundreds of people whom I'd like to thank but I've only got one page to do it. So here are the top few:

My family – Tania, Phoenix, Mum, Dad, David and Janet who always give me such encouragement to be the best at everything I do. Thank you for reading this through and finding all the mistakes for me.

Paul Ergatoudis – owner of the Go Dating Brand and the person who gave me my first opportunities to work in the dating industry.

All my loyal hosts (past and present) who have helped me run hundreds of successful singles events.

John Mulvey and Kirston Winters who constantly nagged me to finish the book. I bet you thought I never would?

Bobby Rakhit – my personal chef, driver and friend. It's a privilege to know you and to see how you've grown over the years.

Josephine Hayes – who got me started on the road to finally getting this completed.

To all the people I met through online sites who allowed me to have so many fun, entertaining and sometimes utterly mad experiences.

Lastly, I want to thank all my dating coaching clients that I've been able to help. You trusted me to change your lives and I'm grateful I was able to make a difference.

I WILL MAKE YOU CLICK

Introduction

"OK, Dating Guru. Can I really meet "the one" through online dating?"

As a dating expert and coach, that's the question that I get asked every day. My short answer is a resounding yes!

According to IbisWorld a leading market research company, the US online dating market is worth over $2 billion dollars. In the UK it makes over £170 million a year and the figure rises dramatically. This is from singles buying memberships on online dating sites. The competition among the sites is huge and they each spend a fortune on advertising to persuade singles that they are the best site to help them find love. More and more sites spring up each week each claiming to be the best and with the most singles on board. If the first one doesn't work, singles can simply sign up to another.

Spending on dating is increasing despite the economic climate. In fact, money spent on online dating is so important to the UK economy that the Office of National Statistics has added online dating to the example basket of goods and services it uses to calculate inflation rates. Most singles have either tried it or are seriously thinking about giving it a go.

So if online dating is so popular with singles then why do so many struggle to make it work?

The simple answer is because it's not as easy as the dating companies make out. There are so many sites out there that it's confusing knowing which one is right for you. When you do narrow it down it can be a frustrating and soul destroying experience. They'd have you believe that all you've got to do is pay them a fee and the other singletons will be beating down your door to meet you. The dating sites love this as once they've got you they know that you'll keep your profile live just in case you miss an opportunity. It's the same as the huge amounts of people who join a gym, only to actually go once or twice. They keep on paying the memberships each month as if that's enough to keep them fit. But it's not a quick fix - if members don't make any effort, they will just be met with silence. Very few people put the effort in and convince themselves they just don't have time.

I do understand this. When I was single I was just the same. I'd often say that I didn't have any time as I worked so much. Sometimes I'd reply that I was too fussy, spent too long hooking other people up instead of giving the time to my own relationships, or that I never really met anyone that I wanted to take out. I'd laugh and say I was enjoying being single and didn't need anyone else in my life. If I was honest with myself, the plain truth is that I wasn't trying hard enough. I realised that I needed to stop making excuses and allow myself to actually accept that I wanted a proper relationship and therefore needed to put the effort in. If you have been single for a while then that's most probably the real reason you are too. In fact, you probably make constant excuses about being too busy, not meeting decent people or that you prefer your own company. Am I right?

Online dating isn't just a fad, it's the future. Dating used to be much simpler many years ago when everyone worked nearby and had family members to hook us up. Today, we all work longer and longer hours and are spread out all over the place. We don't have as much money, time or energy as we'd like to find possible partners. Nightclubs and bars aren't great meeting places due to the noise levels. Most of us are at least a little bit shy and it's hard to go up and approach people we are attracted to. So it's fortunate that the internet has revolutionised dating and magically makes things ridiculously easy. For example, it's now possible to set up an account and begin searching through thousands of singles in your area within minutes. You don't even have to have a shave or touch up your make-up before you chat to them. If you are sat at your computer in just your underwear then nobody need ever know, although there are a few sites that encourage it.

The ever updating technology of mobile phones has only improved the situation. There are so many phone based dating sites and dating apps, with new ones coming out every week. You can chat, flirt and banter with other members who might be many miles away or pinpoint them to the nearest street. I expect that one day these apps will be so advanced you won't even need to do anything other than press a button and meet your perfect match.

When it first started there was a bit of a stigma about saying you met on a dating site and not something you'd admit to if you could help it. That's just because it was new and nobody really knew much about it, so they were wary. It was the same for electricity, the television and iPods when you think about it. The good news is that stigma is long gone and almost all single professionals have tried one form of online dating or another. I expect you will even know some couples who met this way.

I'm going to give you the latest expert information about how to find the love of your life through online dating. I'll show you how to improve your chances, what you should and shouldn't say or do. You'll have a diary rammed full of so many dates that you'll have to turn them away. I'll be taking you with me on an amazing adventure into the secret world of online dating. I have worked for many leading companies from behind the scenes, so I have the advantage of knowing all the insider secrets.

I'll look into as many new dating sites and ideas as I can so you can avoid the bad ones and enjoy the best of them. There are lots of so called online dating guides out there but my aim is to make this the biggest, most useful of them all. I'm going to be including strategies and templates you won't find anywhere else. It's not just theory – it's tried and tested information that has worked for 100s of my personal coaching clients.

Hopefully, once you've finished the book you'll be armed with enough advice and tools to go out and meet the person you've been waiting for all your life. If you aren't single then I hope you still enjoy reading and remember to pass on any tips you can to your single friends. It's not just dating skills that you can improve with my advice. This also applies outside the dating world as it's all about giving things a second look and being happy with what you have. So you can use these tips to make new friends, become fitter, get the job of your dreams, negotiate better and have a much more interesting, powerful life.

I'd like you to consider this book as something you can dip in and out of when you like. Although there are amusing bits, it's not a novel so you won't lose track if you read the chapters in any order you fancy. I've found that some sections are difficult to place as they can apply to more than one area, but hopefully I've included everything you are looking for. You might want to start at the very beginning, which I've had on good authority is a very good place to start. On the other hand, I know some of you will have more internet dating experience than others. You might well have a particular issue that you are facing right now, so feel free to flick right to that bit if you want. I won't mind, I promise. Everyone will be at different stages of their dating lives and looking for different information.

I'm British but I do coach clients all over the word thanks to the wonders of Skype. So while I mainly work with British dating sites, all my advice works with the various worldwide online dating sites that I've worked with too. Many sites are open to anyone, wherever they might be but I've included the best local ones in the appendix at the back of the book. I always keep an up to date list on my personal website too, so you will find it useful to visit this at http://www.jamespreece.com/

My advice applies to everyone, whether you are a teenager or a silver surfer. It makes no difference about the type of person you want to meet or your sexual orientation. What does matter is that you are looking for a serious relationship. I don't teach short term tricks that lead to nothing – I work on long term results.

Please remember that when it comes to dating there are no exact rules as every person and situation is different. So instead, please take my advice only as a guideline that you are free to deviate from whenever you wish. Take responsibility for living the life in the way that makes you happiest – nobody else can do that for you. If you do end up meeting the love of your life then I will of course take all the credit and expect an invite to the wedding.

However, let me be clear about something. Under no circumstances do I suggest that you use your new found powers to mess people around. That's not what this book is about. You deserve to meet someone amazing and I'm going to help you do this.

There's really only one way I can start this book and that's with my own success story. To me, this is my ultimate qualification as the Dating Guru – I took my own advice and won the heart of the woman of my dreams. That's not a boast; it's a gold cup you will get when you win the dating game. It's the prize that makes all the effort, strange dates, time and confusion worth it.

Dating was never easy for me, at least back when I first started. When I was younger, I was never very lucky with women. If I flipped a coin in the air it wouldn't even land on the Queen. I was shy and didn't know how to interact with women. I had a few girlfriends but no clue about what to do with them. At primary school, pulling the girl in front's pigtails was the closest I got to flirting. However, I discovered the power of online dating in the early days of the Internet, back when there were just a handful of sites. I soon noticed that I was getting rather more female attention than I was used to. I worked out exactly what I needed to say and do to get them to want to meet me. I'd spend hours each day chatting to gorgeous women, who seemed to like my playful sense of humour and cheeky grin.

I dated lots of girls and each one brought me a different life experience. Most were lovely and some were utterly mad, but I'll save those stories for another book. With each date I had I knew that I was getting a little better at dating and I learned more about myself with each one. I spent a few years working as an Actor and helped out at a few singles events to make a little extra money. Before too long I was working for all the best Singles Parties companies in the UK, running speed dating and helping the guests mingle with each other. It was by doing this that I learned to study their body language and found out what they were looking for. I heard their struggles with meeting the right partners and the difficulty they had in getting second or third dates.

I spotted a huge gap in the market for a Dating Coach – someone to show them what they needed to do and how exactly they needed to do it. Now it's something I do full time. I write attention getting profiles for my coaching clients and often send out messages on their behalf. I've even been known to watch them on dates (for feedback purposes) and help them approach the people they fancy. As well as this I work with matchmaking and dating companies, helping them make sure their customers have more successful love lives. To date I have run 1000s of singles events, coached 100s of people on a one to one basis all over the world and appear every week in the media. That's why I'm the Dating Guru and that's why I'm the man to help you.

As I mentioned, I did eventually marry my very own Miss Right, so I can assure you that what I'm going to teach in this book really works. I was fortunate to find her and it reinforces my belief that there is someone out there for everyone – as long as you put a plan in action to find them. I was putting myself out there, but ultimately it was my wife that found me.

You might be surprised to hear that it wasn't through the normal online dating sites. It wasn't even through mutual friends. Instead, it was from a little site called MySpace, the free online social networking website.

Although I'd had a couple of dates through Myspace, I'd only really set it up as an Acting Portfolio, with my headshots and performing CV. Tania was "holding out for a hero" and was fed up waiting for him to arrive. She had grown tired of meeting her own selection of oddballs and unsuitable men, so she made a decision to start being more proactive and look at all avenues. One part of this happened when she signed up to Myspace and contacted men she liked the look of. As fate would have it, this included me. We sent a few messages back and forth and agreed we rather liked the sound of it and had lots in common.

I'm proud to say that my years of experience paid off and I persuaded her to meet me for a date. As it turned out I was the first person she ever met from the internet so was understandably a little nervous. I fancied her rotten the second I saw her and took her for a couple of drinks in her village pub. We both wanted to see each other again after our first date. She later told me that my charm had won her over and intrigued her enough to want to find out more about me. Her online dating success rate is 100% which just goes to show that she's perfect in yet another way.

I'm delighted to say that I proposed to her late on a snowy Christmas evening, by the Christmas Tree on her village green after a late night carol service. She agreed on the condition I did so properly, which lead to a very wet knee.

I'm still learning how to be a good partner. Just because we are happily married doesn't mean we are going to stop dating. We just celebrated the 7th anniversary of our first meeting and spent four amazing days together. We had meals out, cooked for each other and went on a chocolate making course among other things. It's very important that when you meet a partner you continue to make time to date. It's too easy to get stuck in a rut, so schedule regular dates and make sure you stick to them. Dating spices up a relationship and gives you the chance to try new things, have fun experiences and you'll always have something to look forward to. When you are dating you'll never get bored or have time to get complacent!

I hope that through this book, each one of you will have your own fairy-tale come true. It's not a happy ending as nothing stops, but only improves. In fact, my life got even better last year when we had a little baby boy. Nothing makes me happier than seeing him laugh and smile. He's already the best flirt I've ever met and never fails to get passers-by to pay him attention.

There's one more thing I'd like to share with you before you begin. I feel I should tell you this now that we're going to be friends. Are you ready? Ok, here's my confession. I'm not perfect. So many "self-help" writers or experts like to give the impression they are infallible and the world magically falls in place around them. I'm just like you. I have my own faults. I have a tendency to daydream and sometimes speak in a very LOUD VOICE. I have a short attention span and get annoyed with people who take advantage of others. The thing is, I accept that these make me the person who I am and am proud of my faults. Work out what yours are and be proud of them too.

Now that's out in the open it's time to begin our journey together and find out where you've been going wrong and how to get an amazing love life. I hope you are ready to take control and work your own magic.

Once you start my online dating master plan you'll see dramatic, life changing results. Please remember to share them with me via my website once you start getting them. There are so many other singles out there who need a little help. It's only through reading and watching success stories that they will know they aren't alone and that they can get what they want too.

If you are ready to start your own Success Story then let's get going. Grab a pen and paper and I'll see you in the next chapter.

Chapter One : Who Do You Want To Meet?

To start things off, I'm going to teach you how to determine EXACTLY what you want in your dating life and help you develop a rock-solid plan for achieving it. We need to first cover something that's more important than choosing a site or what you need to do on it. You see, before you even begin online you need to be clear about the person you want to meet. If you don't know you'll never realise when they come your way

I'd like you to try something for me right now. It's the first part of some life changing techniques that are unbelievably powerful when used together. Don't worry, it's all fun and won't take very long. If you put in a little thought now you'll be ready and prepared for the journey ahead.

So grab yourself a pen and paper or open up a blank document on the computer. If you are like me, you'll probably do the computer version as writing things by hand can seem like hard work nowadays.

Here's the first step:

We need to work out exactly what you want from the dating game.

After all, if you don't know what you want how will you know when you've got it?

If you want a holiday, you wouldn't just get on the first plane that comes and see where it takes you, as fun as that might be. If you want to make a cake or cook a meal you wouldn't just stumble around the supermarket guessing at ingredients. Otherwise you'll end up with a random concoction that might just make you a little bit sick. Instead, you'd write down everything you might want before you head out as well as the exact quantities. You'd know what you don't want to eat and would have an idea of a rough budget too. It's exactly the same when it comes to dating. You don't want to just date anyone as you have your own unique set of tastes and requirements. So you need to make yourself a dating "shopping list."

Stick to the most important things and keep things fairly open. Who exactly do you want to meet? What's important to you? Don't limit yourself. I want you to imagine that you could date absolutely anyone in the world. Well, almost anyone. I don't want you to think about a real person, film star or ex-partner. Some people are tempted to make a lovely list of all the qualities they believe their last partner had. Please don't do this! You broke up for a reason so the last thing you want to do is end up comparing all future dates with them. Those qualities didn't work for you. This is a whole new beginning for you so be open to whoever comes along.

This person will be the dream combination of everything you've ever wanted. What's more, let's pretend you've been dating them for exactly a year now, are both in love and ecstatically happy.

You are sat in a restaurant, waiting for them to arrive and celebrate your one year anniversary together. How are you feeling? Is your heart beating fast from the excitement?

They've walked in now, have spotted you and are making their way over. They smile, you hug/kiss and then they sit down opposite you. You gaze into each other's eyes and all the worries and flickering thoughts melt away.

Picture what they would look like, what they would sound like. Take as long as you want to do this, there's no time limit, just your imagination. How old are they, what colour is their hair? What's so special about them and why do you like them so much? Think about how they smell, how they look at you and what you have in common. If you'd like to, you could also think of some of the memories you share from your first amazing year together.

You'll now be feeling incredibly positive and you'll soon be able to start thinking of the endless possibilities that could happen for you. It's so important that you start this adventure with a clear idea of what you want your end result to be. I do want you to be as open minded as possible but everyone has their own set of "deal breakers" that they know deep down they can never compromise on. So work out now what you'd most like to have and you can use it as a guide. If you spend a little time working things out now you'll be able to know instantly when you've met them!

This is your fantastic opportunity to create your own once in a lifetime Fairy-tale Romance,

I strongly believe in the "Law of Attraction" and that you can use it to your advantage. The Law states that your thoughts and feelings manifest into your reality. Like attracts like and if you are happy and positive you'll meet someone similar. It's all about sending out the right frequencies and attracting back someone who matches them.

This method helped me find my wife. After we'd been dating a few months I happened to look back on my old dating notes. Hidden away was my "Law of Attraction" secret list that I made to ask the universe to bring me my dream woman. Amazingly, Tania fitted all but one of the points on my list. The only thing she didn't match was that she didn't have a pierced belly button. This didn't matter as it wasn't something I wanted anymore. I did go through a phase of finding piercings and tattoos sexy but quickly realised I was attracting the wrong sort of girl.

The dating shopping list has worked for many other people I know. Not just in relationships, but for jobs, money, success and other aspects of everyday life. All I ask is that you try and see how this might be useful to you. At the very least, you'll be thinking positively about things. Positive thoughts breed positive actions and reactions. If you don't agree, think of it in reverse. If you spend your time dwelling on negative things, that's exactly what you are going to end up bringing into your life.

I want you to be really open minded about the person you want to meet, so remember that the longer your list the harder it will be to find someone with all these qualities. I'd suggest that a good list will have about ten items on it. These will be the absolutely vital things. Perhaps they have to be able to make you laugh or who is of the same religion as you. Or you want to meet someone who has a child or lives within twenty miles of you. If these are truly important then you do need to specify them now.

Your list is ready when you can look at it and believe that it's realistic, achievable and something that makes you happy.

If you've done this then so far you are doing brilliantly. So I know you can handle the next really easy step. We have to make a plan and agree to stick to it. Studies show that people who write their goals down are much more likely to achieve them, than just keeping them in your mind.

This isn't just about making a wish list and expecting miracles to occur without taking responsibility. Dreams really can come true but fate sometimes needs a helping hand. Remember that even Cinderella had her Fairy Godmother to help her glam up and go to the ball in order to find her Prince Charming! If she'd sat moping around at home making pumpkin soup then their paths would never have crossed. So I am your Dating Fairy Godfather and now you need to think positively, get yourself online, start looking and you'll find someone soon enough. It's all about taking action which is a subject I'm going to go on about a fair bit in this book.

From then on, our plan will be relatively simple. You just need to state your intentions in an agreement with yourself to make it work. When you write down your intentions on the "contract" put your name on and write it addressed to you. Tell yourself exactly what you want to achieve and how you are going to do it. You'll also need to specify a timescale. There's no point making it too soon or you won't give it enough of a chance and don't make it too far away or you'll procrastinate. Believe me; I know all about procrastination as it's one of my own worst habits. I am a procrastinator with mild OCD so I have a tendency to do nothing over and over and over again. Set yourself a realistic target that you can achieve, somewhere between 6 and 12 months from now.

For example:

> I, Sarah Smith will find a serious partner by June 14th. This is a list of the following 10 qualities my dream man will have. I will join at least one online dating site and contact at least 10 new people every day. I promise to give more men a chance and go out on two different dates a week and will keep going until I meet someone amazing.

If you've written it on a computer then you should print a few copies out. Then all you need to do is sign it.

Once you've made your agreement, put it somewhere that you look often. Perhaps on a mirror, a fridge door or on a post-it note on your monitor. That way you'll subconsciously keep looking at it and absorbing the "list" and you'll ready yourself for when you meet new people. If you are worried you won't be able to stick to it then you could also email a few copies to your closest friends. That way they'll be able to encourage and motivate you. You might want to leave off anything too embarrassing if your friends are anything like mine.

Now that wasn't so hard was it? You've now got something

to aim for and we can work together to make sure you get to achieve the things you've written down. That's once you've learned to forget all the things about dating you think you already know.

Time to break the Rules – Online Dating Misconceptions

When it comes to dating and online dating, there is a lot of very bad information out there. If you run an internet search you can find a virtually unlimited amount of "dating advice." So much of it is conflicting and it's almost impossible to tell what works and what is complete nonsense.

You may have been told about certain dating rules you'll need to follow if you want success. While there are some valid points, most of what you think you know is completely wrong. For example, don't contact someone for three days after they contact you. You may think that you are making it appear that you lead a busy life but they aren't stupid. Instead you just look rude and that you aren't remotely interested in seeing them or their feelings. I'm not saying you should reply back instantly but the longer you leave it then the longer they'll reply to you in return. Leave the game playing to the teenagers. Life is too short and I want you to have quick results. Someone could get in there and snap them up while you are messing around.

The truth is that there are no rules when it comes to dating as every person you meet is completely different. I can give you guidelines and suggestions but being adaptable and making up your own mind are vital skills. Forget the rules and live by your own code of acceptable conduct. Treat people how you'd like to be treated yourself.

It's also amazing how many people still believe outdated misconceptions about online dating. I hear these all the time and it annoys me quite a bit. For example "people on these websites lie about their age, their physique - it is impossible to trust anything anyone says." They use these excuses as reasons not to give it a go and therefore hinder their chances of meeting some lovely people.

Here are some common myths that I'm going to bust for you now:

Isn't Online Dating just full of losers and weirdoes?

Over 70% of singles have tried online dating, so you can't class that many as "weird"! Yes, as with any large mix of people there will be a few oddballs, but overall most online daters are busy professionals who just don't have time to meet people in bars and clubs. You'll meet just as many strange people in the so called "real world" anyway. Have a look at the crowds next time you get on a train or go shopping. At least when you are online you can avoid them if you choose to. Anyone that gives online dating a go is obviously a little more fun and open to adventure than those who don't anyway.

I don't want to put my photo up. What if someone I know sees it?

That doesn't matter, as that means they must also be signed up to the same site, doing the same thing as you anyway. Most people don't have any issue with putting photos up on social media sites and there's no difference when it comes to Online Dating. Don't worry about what anyone else thinks. It's your life and you can do what you want.

What if I get stuck on a date with someone I can't stand?

This is the reason why I suggest you never arrange a drinks or dinner date. Instead, say you are busy and just meet for an hour for coffee. If you don't get on, you can leave. If you hit it off, you can always meet again or "cancel" your other plans! I'll give you some great ways to escape a dodgy date later in the book.

Doesn't everyone lie on their profile?

I'm not going to deny that white lies are common – after all the intention is to present the very best possible version of "you". However, bigger fibs are rare as they are instantly obvious once you do meet. There's no point saying you are 6 foot 2 if you are really 5 foot 5 as you won't get away with it. I'll tell you more about when it's acceptable to stretch the truth a bit later on.

Online Dating is too expensive!

Most online dating sites work out more expensive if you only sign up for one month, but almost all sites can work out much cheaper if you do it over the long term. You really do get what you pay for and you are paying for the security and quality of a safe, monitored database. If you put the cost into perspective, most people are happy to pay for a gym membership or for a theatre ticket, so why not pay a little to boost your love life? It's the best value investment you can ever make if you end up meeting your future partner.

It's not romantic and takes away the magic!

Looking at a screen and typing on a keyboard isn't remotely romantic. The magic comes once you make a connection. It's the butterflies in your tummy as you think about meeting them, the thoughts of a possible future together and the laughs you share getting to know each other. When you finally meet face to face, the romance comes as you plan your dates and enhance your natural chemistry.

You are ultimately responsible for your own decisions in life and for your own love life. So throw away all the ridiculous ideas you've been told and be as open minded as possible.

My Huge Dating Tip: The High Street Test:

Do you think that you are too fussy to find someone you like?

People keep complaining to me that they just can't find anyone they are attracted to. They tell me that they don't meet enough new people or get the opportunity to talk to them. If this is you, please try doing this for me:

Spend ten minutes on a Saturday afternoon walking from one end of your high street to the other. Make sure it's a busy day when there are lots of people about. Start at one end and as you walk along, take a note of everyone you pass. As you walk by, add up how many of these you would be happy to go out on a date with. Keep walking around for ten minutes and then make a note of your tally. Believe me, this soon puts a stop to any ideas you might have about being too picky. I've asked clients to play this game and they always come back to me with staggeringly high numbers. There are plenty of potential dates out there right now. Can you even imagine how many more are online, waiting for you to reach out and say hello?

Are You Ready For Love? Having a Positive Mental Attitude

Hold on, before you begin searching online for people to date, there is a very important thing you need to do. You need to get yourself into the right state of mind! Many people have had bad dating experiences. Perhaps you've been badly hurt, rejected or not been able to get what you want. So you start to believe it's your fault and that you are destined to repeat the same patterns. These limiting beliefs can be caused by memories from childhood. We are products of our environment – our friends, parents and teachers ultimately help shape us into the person we are now. This can make you wary of starting new relationships. So it's time for you to leave the past where it is and concentrate on the future instead. Your beliefs can be changed relatively easily if you work on them, but the events in your past made you the person you are today and you should always be proud of that.

It's not just the past that can stop you from succeeding. Self-sabotaging your love life by staying in an unhappy relationship can hold you back from finding "the one". This is usually because you enjoy the ego boost or would rather be with "anyone" than be alone. Your life has become a series of routines that you do together and you can't imagine going back to being on your own. I can't stress this enough: If you believe that you aren't complete unless you have a partner then this is destructive and you need to change your thinking right away!

Perhaps you've been seeing someone who isn't ready to commit to the relationship. If you want something more long-term and defined then you should work out if they will ever change their minds. If not, you should end things immediately and not waste any more time on them. The same goes for any negative aspect of a relationship, whether it's cheating, verbal abuse or laziness. End it right now. They are simply holding you back from being completely happy. You will never meet Mr or Miss Right if you aren't ready to give them 100% of your love, time or attention. If you have any "special friends" that you see for sex from time to time then you've got to break it off with them too. Sorry, but you do. You can't give yourself physically or emotionally to someone else while you are thinking about another person.

Get rid of any baggage, get shot of your fears and open yourself up to the wonderful new possibilities that will arise. They are waiting for you – you just have to be ready to accept them into your life.

What you have to offer Mr or Miss Right?

How dateable do you think you are? Just because you want to date a certain type of person, doesn't mean they will be interested in you in return. Lots of people fail as they think that just by paying for a dating service, everyone will suddenly start throwing themselves at them. You have to give them a reason to want to get to know you. You are going to have to learn to "sell yourself" with your online dating profile if you want to make it work.

I'm going to be showing you a wide variety of ways to make yourself into a great catch later in this book. But first, we need to work out what's special about you.

It's really not just about looks. It's not even about how rich, successful, young or old you are. Every single person in this world has something unique and wonderful to offer. It will be the thing that everyone comments on. This can be anything from a particular talent to a fantastic smile.

Perhaps you're great with kids or animals adore you. Can you bake amazing cakes? Could you look sexy in a bin bag? Is your Elvis impression out of this world? Do you know the Mexican word for goldfish? Can you remember all the words to long forgotten pop songs? These are all wonderful things that you can write about in your profile.

One of the most commonly heard dating tips is "be yourself" and that's usually very good advice. You must make sure that you are always the best "you" possible. When you go out in your best clothes, make-up and hair you'll instantly become more confident and up your social standing. Confidence is sexy and stands out a mile. However, if you are unhappy and have nothing going on in your life then being yourself clearly isn't enough. The more exciting your life is then the more other people will want to share it with you. So before you start looking for someone to have adventures with, make sure you are already having lots of your own. If your free time is spent watching television and collecting crisp packets then you are probably going to have to shake things up a bit. For example, we've all got a secret hobby that we'd like to try. Find out what is on in your area and put your name down for a few things.

Here are a few ideas:

Salsa dancing

Cooking classes

Art classes

Chocolate Making

Martial Arts

Photography

Creative Writing

Walking Groups

Wine Tasting

Computer Skills

Try and think outside the box. The more exciting your hobbies are then the more other people will want to hear about them and be interested in you. It's wonderful to try new things and also good to test yourself by getting out of your comfort zone a little every now and again.

If you are a shy person, then I'd definitely suggest you seek out your local amateur dramatics group. There are usually several in each area and they are desperate to find new members to appear in the shows. I'm not suggesting you immediately take the lead in "My Fair Lady" or "Mother Goose." To start with, a small part with a few lines will make a huge difference to your confidence levels. You'll make new friends and will have long lasting memories to look back on.

All these activities, societies and groups are also potential places to meet someone so that's a fantastic bonus. If nothing more then you'll make some new friends and they might have someone they can introduce you to.

You must find things that you are passionate about and also start to think about what you want in life. Passion and ambition are very sexy things. It doesn't really matter **what** you are passionate about, but if you can talk about something with great delight and enthusiasm it's naturally going to be infectious. Try and be as happy as you can every single day. Once you are living a full, positive life then everyone will be falling over themselves to be with you.

Important: My clients often tell me that they are looking to find their other half, or for someone to complete them. I hate these terms as they suggest they aren't enough which is nonsense. So before we work together, I want you to know this: You are perfect just as you are. You don't need someone else to validate you.

That may sound a strange comment to write in a dating book, but it's important that you accept that to be true. Having a partner, wife, husband, lover, boyfriend or girlfriend is a truly wonderful thing and life is more exciting with someone to share it with. I just want you to love yourself first. If you don't then you can't expect anyone else to.

You are now in a much better place to begin online dating. Let's get started.

Chapter Two : Choosing the Right Website

The Online Dating industry is growing so fast that hundreds of new websites spring up each and every week. There really is quite a ridiculous number or sites and it's more and more difficult for singles like to you to tell them apart. The majority of these are standard "dating" sites but the companies have realised the best way to get new members is to be really specific about who they target.

So there are now websites for just about every possible niche. The simplest ones are for regular dating sites based on religion, eating habits, lifestyle or hobbies. Then they can get even more complicated. Do you want to only date a nudist, giant or millionaire pensioner? There are sites out there for you. In fact, there's probably even a site out there for those who want to date giant nudist millionaire pensioners. If there's not then you can set up your own in just minutes. Check out the appendix at the end of this book if you'd like to know more about that.

Other mainstream, non-dating related companies are also jumping on the bandwagon and launching their own branded dating sites. So you'll see high street clothes shops, fitness magazines or restaurants all advertising that they have the hottest new dating site.

The idea is to get you to sign up to as many websites as you can afford, in the hope that you'll assume each site is different.

Here's the secret. Many of these niche sites (with some exceptions) are what are known in the trade as "white label sites." This means that they are carbon copies of each other. There are a couple of big players out there who are responsible for thousands and thousands of these sites.

The best way to understand how this all works is to imagine a large party in an infinite sized venue. Everyone is inside having fun, but they want to keep meeting new faces. So the party organisers offer promoters a share of the ticket entry price in return for getting these new faces inside. The promoters don't have to do any of the party organising or issues that might come with it. Each promoter advertises their own "special" party that is aimed at a particular crowd. Once a ticket is bought, they get to go through their unique front door into the venue.

However, once they've been in the venue for a short while they soon realise that they are still able to meet everyone else in the venue. It's one massive shared database with lots of different ways in. This is brilliant as it means you are going to have a huge number of singles available to you. The downside is that you must be very careful that you aren't paying twice for exactly the same thing. I've heard of people who have signed up to five or six sites like this before they realised what was happening.

So which site should you sign up to? Go to the one that you've heard most about or the one you've seen advertised everywhere. If you know about it then everyone else will too and this means a large database of members. Always start with one of the big mainstream sites and go niche later if necessary. If you are completely new to dating then my website has a list of the very best sites that I recommend. The good ones that are full of potential and can really work for you. If you have friends who have tried online dating ask for their thoughts too, but pay more attention to the positive comments they give. If it didn't work out for them then perhaps they just had the wrong strategy like most people.

TOP TIP: It's not just these white label sites that share databases. The two major players in the UK – Match.com and Dating Direct are run by a company called Meetic and if you are a member of one you can sign in to the other. In fact, you can even sign in to their overseas site Meetic.com too. Very few people know this.

Not all dating sites are white label and there are plenty of dedicated Niche ones with unique databases. I'll list the best ones at the end of this book, along with some special strategies you can use.

Things can get even more complicated. As well as sites that you have to pay for, there are a growing number of free ones too. But are they a good way for you to get dates?

Free Dating or Scams?

Online Dating can be expensive, so free sites can be a good introduction if you can't afford this. However, they are more suited to casual hook ups and flirting than serious relationships. If you are over the age of 21 then you'll probably be wasting your time even setting up a profile.

The users of these sites are much less likely to put any effort. The result is shorter introduction messages such as "Hi, you look fit" and "How are you?" Completely pointless and very irritating, especially as most of these are unsuitable matches.

Free dating sites are not as commonly monitored for fake profiles and there are many time wasters on there. You get men posing as girls and girls pretending to be boys. If someone gets removed it's easy to create another profile and sign right back on again. They are the playground of the Scammers and the Catfish and you can read more in the chapter later in the book.

I've softened to these free sites a little more as I can see there are some benefits as long as you are extra careful. Put in the hard work to create a profile on a paid site and then copy it for a free one, just to see if you get any interest. Don't spend too much time using it but see if anyone naturally contacts you. Use some common sense to check they are real and don't be naïve. If you have a two line profile and no photo but are suddenly bombarded with interest immediately then something is wrong.

Most of these types of websites are never as "free" as they make out. While you can search and contact members, you still need to upgrade and pay for some of the more useful services. This could be to find out if someone has read your message, to see who might be interested in you or to get your profile promoted over others. These sites have to make money somewhere. As well as the upgrade options, you'll see adverts on every page. This is no big deal, but it's easy to get distracted.

I would always advise that if you are looking for a long term relationship then you are better off paying for a proper online dating site. You know the other person is serious about dating if they have also paid. They attract many more professional members and therefore you'll meet more suitable people.

A good, reputable online dating site (such as the ones at the end of this book) will have teams of staff who are always available to help you. They will filter out fake profiles and ensure that the quality of members is kept as high possible. If you have any sort of problem or need help they will get back to you quickly with a solution.

While I don't think free sites are great right now, I expect the balance may shift over the coming years. More "Freemium" dating sites will pop up due to the rise in free dating apps so the big players will have to compete. I'll go into this in more detail later in the book, but it's not important to you at this moment in time. For now, just remember that you get exactly what you pay for. I want you to put your effort into using a paid online dating site.

TOP TIP: Ignore the reviews. Just because a site has terrible reviews, doesn't mean it's bad. This is because the people who get married rarely share their good news. It's just the few unhappy people who make the most noise and want to vent about it. Instead, ask your single friends about their own experiences. Chances are that they would have plenty of stories to tell you to guide you to the right site.

The Best Time of Year to Sign up to a Dating Site

There is one absolute peak time for the dating industry. This is the week before Christmas, right up until just after Valentine's Day. That's approximately mid-December to mid-February which gives you a two week hotspot. The reason for this is simple – it's when many people are ready to make a new start or stick to a new year's resolution. It's the same time that everyone signs up to gyms or decides they want to quit smoking. Singles want to find someone once and for all and they know the pressure is on to find a Valentine quickly.

Winter has cold dark longer nights so are lots more people online. The Summer is also a great time for online dating, but it can vary depending on what the weather is doing. We tend to be in a happier, more positive mood when the sun shines and are keen to make the most of the longer nights.

If you are reading this book at other times of the year, then don't panic! There are definite advantages to using them at other periods and the sites are rarely quiet. Firstly, you are more likely to be sent discount offers to persuade you to pay up. You'll also find the members are more likely to be interested in you as there is less competition and you'll be a new face.

If you get your profile ready in the quieter times of the year then it will be ready to entice the new members when they appear. You'll also have had time to learn the ropes and how everything works, giving you a head start of the new joiners.

Making Payment

Don't make any sort of payment until your profile is perfected, your photos are approved and you understand how the site works. When you pay then you'll unlock features that will only be a distraction at this point. You won't want anyone looking at a half-finished profile either as they might never come back for a second look. Pay when you are absolutely ready and everything is in place.

Optional Extras and Upgrades - Are they Worth Paying for?

Most sites, even the free ones, still need to make money. So they are coming up with more and more Premium features to help you have a better experience on the site. You'll be pushed into upgrading to these right after your initial payment (when you are in purchasing mode) and every time you log in afterwards. For example you could pay extra to:

See who has read your message

Allow non-paying members to read your message or contact you

Send a virtual gift such as a cartoon teddy bear or glass of imaginary wine

Get your Profile first in the search results or highlighted in newsletters

Attend exclusive singles events at a discount

These are all quite useful features to have but they are no means essential to your success. If you have the money to spare, it may be worth trying some of these out just to see if it improves your chances. You'd probably be better off using the money to get some professional photographs instead. That would be your best investment.

How long should you sign up for?

It would be wonderful if you could sign up to an online dating site for a couple of weeks and then meet the love of your life. While this book will obviously dramatically increase your chances, you aren't going to like everyone you go on a date with. So don't expect this process to take less than six months. That may seem like a long time, but it will go much faster than you expect. Even if you date two people every week, you may find that you have gaps in between your hard work where you go on holiday or have short relationships.

Most dating sites let you join on a monthly, three monthly or six monthly basis. While the longer period is the most expensive, it works out much cheaper than paying month by month. So if you are completely new to online dating, go with a six month commitment to start with. It's better to focus all your efforts on using just one site as it will take a little while to get used to it. If you've had a go before, then you may prefer to try two different sites, each for three months.

One month memberships tend to lead to you being either overwhelmed or disappointed. If you go for a six month deal and then meet someone after two then it will have been an incredibly worthwhile investment, so there's nothing to lose.

Now it's time to tell you something that dating sites don't want me to share with you. It could save you more than the cost of this book alone, so you really don't want to skip this bit!

You MUST read the terms and conditions of your membership very clearly. You'll think that you are only under contract for the length of time you selected, but you could end up with a nasty shock. The majority of dating sites will repeat bill you on the term you've selected. This is always written on the payment page but many people are in such a hurry that they'll miss it. If you get charged and don't want it then there is very little you can do to get a refund.

This may seem like a very sneaky and underhand tactic and to many people it's completely unfair. Even as a leading Dating Expert, I initially struggled with the morality of it all. I could see how a member might feel ripped off but it costs a dating site more to acquire a customer than the money they'd make from a 6 month membership. That's because of the huge amount they have to spend on advertising to make you aware their site exists in the first place. They need to tie them in for a longer period of time – much like a gym or television subscription service – to make it worth operating at all. If they didn't do that, the initial cost would have to be a great deal higher. The sites that didn't repeat bill wouldn't make enough money to compete with the sites that did and they would soon go under. I can see both points of view so as long as repeat billing is made absolutely crystal clear then I see it as a necessary part of the process. The industry is becoming much more transparent as time goes on which is a good thing. This doesn't mean you need to tie yourself in to an endless run of memberships you don't need though.

Make a note in your diary, set an alarm in your phone or send yourself a timed email to log in about a week before the renewal date. You are responsible for this so you can't blame the site if you don't take control yourself.

If you are enjoying the site, then you may well be perfectly happy to continue using it. If you would like to give it a rest and try another site, then by all means cancel your membership. While you run the risk of losing your discounted rate if they increase in the future, you'll probably be inundated with "come back" offers for a long time afterwards. Some of these rates may be cheaper than the price you paid in the first place. If you think you might need this, don't be tempted to delete your profile. If you do that then there's no going back. If your profile is kept live then you can keep dipping in and out on a few sites every three months or so. You can swap between them and contact any new people who have joined since you were last on. You'll probably see quite a few unanswered messages, winks and favourites that you can get started on.

TOP TIP: Even if a website doesn't send you a special offer, there's no harm in asking them if they can give you one. Ask as politely as possible as demands or suggestions you can get a better deal elsewhere are just rude. Tell them you'd love to try the site out but can't afford much at the moment. Can they do anything to help? This doesn't always work if you've not had a previous membership, but there's no harm in asking anyway. Keep in mind that if you do take a trial or discount, it may renew after the agreed time at the full rate once again.

Getting Started

When you've chosen the site that you'd like to sign up to then you are ready to get moving. You'll start by entering all your basic information, such as your email address, date of birth, height, location and some rough details about your hobbies and interests.

Now I know what you are thinking: I'll shave a few years off my age or add a few inches on to my height. Yes, it might get you a little more attention but once you get found out (and you will) then it will only lead to disappointment. You've misled them and are trying to start a relationship based on a lie. This will mean instant rejection and even if you get on they will find it hard to trust you again. Not the best start, I'm sure you'll agree.

Age is the most common thing that people will lie about, whether it's with online dating or in real life. The average age gap in marriages is with the man being three to seven years older than the female. There are always exceptions but that's generally the pattern. Men will chase after younger women, but women generally look better as they age. Many men will lose their hair, put on weight or forget how to dress – especially if they have been in a long term relationship. Women on the other hand are much more likely to eat healthier, exercise more and have the added benefit of being able to wear makeup. This leads to the problem that men are ruling out the women they meet and the women aren't interested in men their own age or above.

When I run my dating events I get calls on an almost daily basis from people who are outside the age limits, but still wish to attend. They will swear blind that they don't look their age and everyone thinks they are much younger. I've never had someone tell me they look their age or older. Funny that. If you really are lucky enough to appear younger then that will be obvious in your photograph. That's in your recent photograph, not one from twelve years ago that you've found at the bottom of your wardrobe.

Be proud of your age, height and things you can't do anything about. If you are unhappy about your weight or job then it's never too late to get down the gym or try something more exciting. You've only got one chance at life and it's way too short to be unhappy.

You will be asked about your body type, but you won't have to enter an exact weight if you don't wish to. The dating site won't want to scare you off, so the choices are usually quite vague – ranging from Slender to Sporty to Average to a Few Extra Pounds. The majority of people can get away with Average but if you are bigger a Few Extra Pounds is perfectly acceptable. If you are in doubt or much larger than Average don't tick any option at all. Your photos will show your body type so it will be clear enough. Please remember that everyone likes different things and we all prefer different body types too. One person may go for a lean, toned look but another will desire a partner with something to cuddle!

While lying is out, do feel free to big yourself up a little. After all, everyone else will be doing the same. If you have a dull job title then you can spice it up a little. Put a word such as Executive or Specialist at the start and you instantly sound much more important. IT and Teaching are two of the most common professions on dating sites so you can get creative to stand out. You could be an Associate Training Executive or a Learning Facilitator rather than a Help Desk Worker or Primary School Teacher. Your title needs to be fun and if it sounds a little bizarre it's an easy icebreaker.

Hobbies and interests: These are essential things you need to specify. You want to sound as exciting and adventurous as possible. It's better to tick plenty of the more ordinary ones (reading/ watching movies/ going to restaurants) than selecting nothing and coming across as being boring. Nobody wants to date a lazy person either, so include lots of physical activities. If you aren't that keen on the gym then maybe you like dancing or going for walks instead.

Income: I don't believe the amount of money you earn should ever be a factor in the type of person who you date. If you are a millionaire or struggling to make a living, that should have no effect on your love life. Unfortunately there are a few people who only search for high earners in the hope this will improve the quality of their own lives. You don't want to date a money grabber so don't give them that sort of information. If a site asks what your income is then be vague and just enter a figure or statement that signals "enough."

Attractiveness: Beauty is in the eye of the beholder, so even if you are extremely attractive it's best not to tell the world you think so. That will make you sound egotistical or vain. Not everyone is secure with their own looks so they might assume you'll never be interested in them anyway. Instead, let your photo be the deciding point for the viewer. There's no point ticking the "You be the judge" or "See my photo" type options either though. Many people will be specifically ticking the "Attractive" and "Average" buttons on their search filters and anything less will never be seen.

Body Type: Most people can get away with "average" or better. If you are outside this bracket then that's fine as long as you are honest. But keep in mind many people will eliminate certain body types when they run searches. If you aren't getting many views then you can leave it blank and show your body type through photos instead. You'll get more hits that way as you won't get filtered out in searches.

Marital Status: If you've previously been married then you definitely need to mention it. You can't try and gloss over it as it's part of who you are and your life story. Tick the divorced or separated box, depending on your situation. To some people, being married shows maturity and proof someone once trusted you to be a good partner. If you've never been married then of course you need to select single.

Children: If you have children, you MUST mention it to rule out all the people who wouldn't be interested. It saves both your time and theirs. If you don't have kids and hope to have one someday then you should mention this here instead. Not everyone wants a family and some won't want to take on someone else's. This is absolutely fine and you have to respect their personal life choices so be truthful.

The next section may ask you to fill in some details about the type of person you want to meet. Leave this as blank as possible to maximise your opportunities. If you start being too strict and putting exact heights, income and so forth then you may find your profile is shown to a lot less people. Take a look at your deal breaker list again and include these things only. For example, if you absolutely would never date a smoker then do tick the non-smoker box. The place to write about your ideal partner is in your profile text as it's much easier to explain there rather than tick a few generic boxes.

Most sites will require you to fill in a minimum percentage of these details. If you don't then you'll get a pop up message asking you to complete them every time you log in. In some cases your profile won't be live or visible until it's up to a high enough standard. This is a wise move as it eliminates low quality and badly written profiles.

You may see other tick boxes in this area, where you can agree to be featured in newsletters or other marketing channels. It's worth saying yes to this as the more exposure you get the better. This is always just for member to member so you won't suddenly find your photo appearing on a poster at a bus shelter.

Once you've got everything completed, you are ready to write your profile. You may wish to have a walk round the block and clear your head before you read the next chapter.

Chapter Three : Creating an Irresistible Profile

How would you like to have an online dating profile that gets you dates even when you are asleep? One so powerful that people will write to you just to comment on how amazing it is? In this chapter I'm going to teach you my Perfect Dating Profile Formula. This is a step by step plan to make sure your profile is the very best it can possibly be.

The sad reality is that most people don't spend long enough writing their profile. It's just not enough to write two lines or make the same generic statement that everyone else does. It can get very boring having to read lots of dull, vague profiles that don't add any value.

Your profile is your sales pitch and your chance to sell yourself in the best light possible. It's your opportunity to beat your competition, so you have to make it count. If you don't, you won't get any interest and will be lost in the sea of other mediocre profiles. Imagine you are buying a car. Which of these two adverts would grab your attention the most?

"Blue car for sale. Runs quite well. Don't really want to sell her but I need the money so I can go on holiday"

Or

"I'm selling my gorgeous Sky Blue car - Betsy. She's been an

amazing companion for some wonderful adventures and has never let me down. I'm travelling overseas so I won't be able to give her the attention she deserves. If you want to take her for a spin then get in touch now and I'll introduce you"

Hopefully you can see how much better the second advert is. A little spark and fun can make you sound like a much better prospect and a person worth meeting. You are the product that you are advertising and you want to ensure you have lots of people wanting it….longing for it….begging for it.

Before we get to your main profile text then there are a few other sections you have to complete first. These are really easy but a few minutes thought on them will make a real long term difference for you.

Choosing a Powerful Username

One of the first things you'll be asked to do when you join a dating site will be to create a username or nickname for yourself. This is the name you'll be known as on the site and the one thing that will make you unique from everyone else. If you get this wrong you can end up ruining your chances before you even start.

It's something lots of people rush through and then end up regretting afterwards. I've seen people give themselves the most ridiculous usernames as they don't realise it's that important. They end up being forever known as "Teapot", "Baby Bird" or "TheDude". (Yes, these are real members on dating sites.) Not the most attractive or interesting I'm sure you'll agree.

This is your chance to get the other member's attention for the right reasons. The better the username then the more interest you're going to get. Having said that it's not something you need to spend hours deliberating. It's more important that you choose something you are comfortable with and happy to be associated with. If you wouldn't be happy wearing it on a badge and walking round with it all day then don't choose it. It needs to be memorable, fun and show a little imagination. Stay away from anything that might be considered controversial, sexual or offensive. "WellhungDon" and "DeadGran" ,I'm talking about you.

Keep it to just three words or under and relatively short. Nothing boring or obvious like "SingleGirl" or "LonelyOne" The best usernames are those with a mysterious and romantic twist, but anything that conveys your personality is fine. Think about your interests, hobbies and job and use them for ideas. Don't worry about being cheesy as it may make people smile and break the ice. If you love working out then you may go for "GymBunny" or if you collect watches then" NickofTime" could be right for you.

On a popular site you're going to struggle to find a name that's original and not already taken. So the site may suggest an alternate name with a long number on the end. I wouldn't suggest you agree to this as it can be confusing to anyone look at it. The only exception would be to use the year you were born. "MoonliteMax77" is much preferable over "MoonliteMax_71841". I wouldn't do this if you were born in 1969 though as that can have a very mixed response!

I often get asked if it's okay to use your real name as your username. I'd say yes, absolutely and it's something I actively encourage. Not your full name of course, but your first name should definitely be part of it.

This will make you seem like a real person rather than someone hiding behind a computer screen.

Here are some great suggestions that you can use for inspiration. Try and think up your own one though as it should something personal to you alone:

NewYorkNelly

GreenEyedGirl

TravelChick

Happy2MeetYou

Brunette Bombshell

FitFriendlyFrank

Siductive

Your Headline

The next task for you is to write a "headline" This is like the title of a book and is simply a few lines to introduce yourself.

Many people don't realise how important this is and rush through it quickly. They assume that the important bit is what you write in your profile, so they write something generic and boring. I want to teach you that if you get it right it's actually a really potent tool to make you stand out.

Some dating sites are now putting less focus on headlines and even removing them altogether. They'd rather you launched right into your profile text. You still should write one anyway and it's the perfect introduction to your profile.

If you were to log in to a dating site right now I'm willing to bet that if you ran a quick search, you'd see that most profiles have a headline much like these:

"Looking to meet new people, have fun and let my hair down"

"Young, Free and Single"

"Happy Go Lucky Lady seeks Romantic Friendly Guy."

"A perfect man for the right woman"

"I can't believe I'm doing this"

"29 year old sociable and easy going girl looking for a likeminded guy"

"Single lady looking for fun and chilled times"

I know this to be true, because I've just done the same test myself. A good 90% of people either write dull, vague or pointless headlines OR can't be bothered to write one at all.

What did you honestly think when you read those examples? Did they make you think, "Wow, they sound perfect for me?" I look at them and wonder why they thought they were a good idea. If you aren't free, single, sociable, easy going, fun, happy etc then you have no hope of meeting anyone.

If you've got an amazing photo, a headline isn't quite so important. If you don't, you need to put the effort in to boost your chances.

So now you will appreciate that a good headline will get lots more people clicking and reading your profile. Here is a list of the very best openers I've seen so you can get an idea of what to write yourself.

I'm not listing these just for you to copy them, but as ideas to spark your imagination. Once people get wind of these then they'll all start using them so they won't have the same effect. So think outside the box and see if you can come up with something just as creative.

1) Is this Ebay? I'm up for auction – highest bidders only!

2) New girl on the block needs a tour guide

3) Can I ask you for directions?

4) Fabulous people deserve to be together, don't you think?

5) Towns yet to be visited, friends in need yet to be discovered, battles yet to be fought…

6) I knew you wouldn't be able to resist!

7) 94.5% of all statistics are fabricated

8) This is really just shopping for guys – two of my favourite things combined!

9) Experimental cook needs food taster

10) Where's "Clever Opening Lines for Dummies" When You Need It?

11) Smart Sexy and Secure

12) Let's dance in the rain

The Perfect Profile Formula

As I promised, I'm now going to teach you how to write a tantalising profile.

This will take more time than anything else but once you've done it you can leave it to work its magic. The more effort you put in now then the more interest and dates you will get.

There is a simple "Five Step" Dating Guru Formula that you just need to follow. I'm going to break it down into very small steps for you:

Step One: Your Headline

Step Two: Opener

Step Three: About You

Step Four Write About the Person You are Looking For

Step Five: End on an invitation

Step One: Your Headline

You've hopefully already written this after reading the earlier section, but if not you should include it now as the start of your profile. This is your chance to get their attention.

Step Two: Opener

First things first – who are you and what are you doing on the site? This is your chance to capture their imagination and get their attention. If this bit isn't good then they'll get bored and won't read any further. Keep it short and simple – it's a taster not a life history.

Step Three: About You

The second part of your profile needs to be your "advert" where you get to sell yourself. Write about what you like doing, what you have to offer and why people should be interested in dating you. Why are you different from all the other people on the site?

Use confident, optimistic language.

You can talk about your proudest achievements but it's important that you aren't boastful. A recent study published by the Journal of Positive Psychology revealed that the character trait that gets people the most interest is humility. They created lots of sample profiles and asked university students to rate the ones that were most dateable. The most humble ones got much higher ratings than the ones that were trying too hard to show off.

Step Four About the Person You are Looking For

Work out what's most important to you and what you want in a partner. Don't be tempted to make a list of things you **don't** want. This just makes you look like a negative person.

When you write this, talk directly to the reader and it will build a stronger connection to their subconscious. Rather than writing statements like "My ideal man is strong and funny," you will have better luck with "You are strong and funny."

Step Five: End on an invitation

This is one of the most important sections. Give the reader the opportunity to get in touch. Ask a question or invite them to suggest something. Don't be boring and play it safe with "Get in touch" or "Drop me an email" as that's not enough. It's better than nothing but you have to use more imagination.

One final tip for you.   Don't be tempted to write too much. People have busy lives and want to be able to get a quick idea of what you are like and who you are. You can save in depth debates and three page anecdotes for when you meet! It should be long enough to reel them in, but short enough to intrigue them.

The Hook

When you are looking at profiles and find one you like, you naturally want to find something you can comment on. You're looking quickly to see if you have anything in common and for a way to break the ice. If you are reading a bland, generic or very short profile then it can be impossible to find anything. This is incredibly frustrating! It confuses your brain and makes it too hard to deal with, so you move on to the next person instead.

That's exactly what everyone else is doing but the solution is easy. Your job is to make it as quick and easy as possible for a person to get in touch. When you write your profile try and fill it with plenty of "hooks" and "bait" to get them contacting you. Write surprising things they won't expect and show off your wonderful sense of humour.

Bonus Dating Tip for Men

Women and men think completely differently so you have to adjust your writing style to adapt. If you want to attract a woman, you have to appeal to their emotional side and paint a mental picture. Tell them about the lovely things you are going to do, such as wandering hand in hand through vineyards and sampling the delicious grapes together.

Bonus Dating Tip for Women

Men will pay more attention to your photo than your profile, but it's still important. We tend to be more rational and logical than women so we look for warning signals.

A man wants a woman to look good on his arm and take care of him. They certainly don't want to be nagged, made to feel small or have to spend their lives pandering to you. So no demands please or negative comments….

Things you Must Never Say!

I'm going to be focusing on some of the very worst things you can put in your profile. These are genuine comments that I see each and every day, over and over. I'll tell you what they are and explain quickly why writing them can be a VERY bad idea:

1)*"Timewasters need not apply"*   You aren't inviting people to view a car, but to meet you. This gives the impression that you've had some bad experiences in the past and are therefore judging all people before you've given them a chance. It's doubtful that anyone would ever admit to being a time waster anyway. Don't be bossy, but try and come across as warm and friendly.

2) *"I can't believe I'm doing this"* This shows instant negativity which is a big turn off to most people. You are suggesting that you are embarrassed to be on the site and therefore hinting you are embarrassed to be contacting them.

3) *"I'm not going to say what I want, but what I DON'T want!"* Writing a long list such as "Nobody under 6ft" or "Nobody who takes themselves seriously" displays instant negativity. Why not spend the time writing about what you do like, rather than what you don't.

4) *"You'll be paying!"* Are you just after them for their money? Never write this, even if it's just as a joke.

5) *"I give great massages"* Do you really? We haven't even spoken yet and you are already getting overtly sexual. Bad idea!

6) *"I am a funny, clever person with a good sense of humour"* The irony of this is that funny, clever people would never write this in their profile – instead they would write something funny and clever!

7) *"Ask me for photo"* You clearly can't be bothered to put one up so why should anyone be bothered to ask?

8) *"Hello how are you?"* This is just incredibly dull, especially if it doesn't lead on to something wonderfully interesting.....and they rarely do.

9) *"Lol!"* You aren't a teenager; you are a successful, intelligent adult, so never write things like this. You must always avoid text speak and demonstrate you can spell properly.

10) *"I'm not a paying member"* So why are you even on the site? You should be embarrassed to look so cheap. Would you sit outside a gym and tell everyone you aren't going to pay but you expect to still get fit? This sort of comment guarantees automatic suspension so never ever write it!

11) *"Good luck with your search!"* I absolutely hate this and it pains me that I'm seeing it increasingly often. In other words, you obviously won't like me so you might as well stop reading now and look for someone you might fancy!

12) *"I like going out and enjoying a bottle of wine or staying at home with a DVD"* 90% of people seem to write this in their profile and it astounds me how commonly used it is.

13) *"I'm equally at home wearing a ball gown and heels or a tracksuit and trainers"* Again, most women write this and think they are being original.

14) *"My friends and family are important to me"* Isn't this really just stating the obvious? Friends and family are important to

everyone. It would be much more worrying and abnormal if they weren't!

15) *"I'm open minded"* While most people write this with the intention that they have no expectations when it comes to dating, the reality is that it comes across as if you looking for a casual relationship.

16) *"I don't know what to write"* or *"I'm not sure what to say."* So you are indecisive and boring right? Of course you aren't....so never write this. Instead carefully write something that will peak their interest and make you sound like someone they'd like to meet.

Personality Forms and Quizzes

Some dating sites have long personality forms and quizzes that you can complete to supposedly help you get more targeted matches. These can take over an hour to compete and will just suck away your valuable time, so are best avoided.

There is an exception to this rule. If you are specifically signing up to a personality based dating site (such as Eharmony or Parship) then you do have to complete these tests. If you don't then you won't be allowed to make your profile live.

Matchmaking software aims to examine members' core beliefs and characteristics to give them a reliable idea of the type of people they should be dating to get a long lasting relationship. But do they really work?

I believe that this sort of profiling might well be useful, but is most probably flawed due to two well know psychological effects.

Barnum Effect: The problem with any form of test is that people are rarely honest about themselves. The Barnum (or Forer effect) is the idea that individuals will give high accuracy ratings to descriptions of their personality that they believe are specifically for them, but are in fact general enough to apply to a variety of different people. So if you give someone the results of a personality profile then they'll choose to accept the bit they like or overlook the ones they don't.

Placebo Effect: If you tell someone that they have been matched with the very latest state of the art findings then they'll subconsciously find themselves working hard to fill in the gaps. This may or may not be a good thing. On one hand, they'll put more of an effort into making a relationship work. On the other it doesn't really matter whether your matches are real or not.

I honestly don't know how accurate these tests really are and nor does any Scientist or Psychologist. From my experience, the secret of successful dating is all about chemistry. There are obviously certain things that are vital when it comes to matching, such as things like race, beliefs, age etc. However, most people have relatively open minds and will be surprised by who they actually really do get on with.

Example Profiles

I'm going to include a few example profile descriptions that I've personally tested out. They are here just to give you inspiration to think of something yourself, not to be copied and pasted word for word. As soon as they get overused then the magic will be lost. Think for yourself and make your own profile a snapshot about YOU and why you are the one they should be dating.

I don't follow every rule I've given you, but I do follow them most of the time. Each one is a roughly similar length which is just about how long you should make sure yours is. There's nothing too serious in the profiles but each is written with just enough to get the reader interested.

The "Are you Ready" Profile

Headline: Live passionately in everything you do.

There are tons of profiles online, decisions can be made in split seconds, depending on the instinct, time of the day, good/bad stories you've just heard today.... you name it.

I am not a particular type, but I'm someone with an open mind, a creative streak and a great sense of humour.) I'm always looking to explore new things or ideas. I can perhaps be a little over emotional at times but I do have an inner peace and relish life

As much as I enjoy my job, I've now reached a stage where I realise that there is so much more to life than working.

I'm also very sporty; I love all sorts of activities - dancing, golfing, skiing etc. I'm passionate about travelling too. I'm Dutch but I've been in the UK for 8 years as I love it here so much.

I'm looking for someone who enjoys life as much as me, trying new experiences and making new memories. You know what you want (both socially and career-wise), and you are positive, kind and up for exciting new adventures together.

It's lovely when a partner looks for small ways to make you happy. Making you smile, ready to be there for each other, to surprise and to share each moment.

I don't have rules and expectations. I'd rather meet up for a coffee sooner rather than later so we can see if the chemistry is there.

So if you are a man who likes to take control and prefers to chat/meet rather than sending out winks please do get in touch right now

The "Christian Grey" Profile.

I put together this to capitalise on the popularity of 50 Shade of Grey. I was curious to find out if women really did want a strong, alpha male like the central character of these books.

I was shocked at the results. I had women throwing themselves at me and many offering to meet up and indulge my fantasies after only a few messages. I even tested it twice – once with an average photo and once with a model one. This made little difference. It was so powerful I had to delete it after a week as I didn't want to mislead anyone or get their hopes up.

It works because it's different to the type of profiles everyone else is writing.

Headline: Looking for my Miss Steele

I'm hardworking, ambitious individual with high expectations of myself, who is also family oriented but with a modern look on life. I am adventurous and outgoing, caring, confident and I take pride in my appearance.

I like socialising, movies, reading, cooking and maintaining a healthy lifestyle by eating well and going to the gym...anything else.. please feel free to ask!

What am I looking for?

I want to make your dreams come true.

I'm looking for someone who will not only be my life partner but my best friend, I want a woman who I can share anything with. Physical attraction is a must, I don't want someone who controls me, I am who I am.

You make me look at the world differently. You don't want me for my money. You give me... hope

Dream of me x

Hearts and flowers?—That's not who I am.   Wine and meal first, to feel that spark.

The Geek Magnet Profile

Headline: There's always cheese on my mousetrap

I'm a positive thinking chap with a very dry sense of humour that is also typically British with a self-deprecating and ironic tendency.

I'm a creative type, happiest when doing all the things that make me feel good, such as travelling, reading, cooking, sleeping on crisp white sheets. Running through Regents park, preferably at 5 in the afternoon on a Sunday with the sun beaming down on my face. Oh, and strong espresso and the pursuit of knowledge.

I can't claim to be much of an 'alpha male' (whatever that means), but I can guarantee that I'm comfortable in my own skin, can take control and make decisions quickly.

I keep an open mind about new opportunities.

Don't you find that the more chances you take the more enriching your experiences are? I keep a close circle of friends and believe passionately in being loyal.

I would like to meet a very special kind of woman who knows what she wants and isn't afraid of new adventures.

You are intelligent, funny, chilled out, communicative, adventurous, kind, gentle, feminine, tactile, spontaneous, classy but not pretentious, sexy and a touch flirtatious. You also like to be spoiled a little every now and again.

Does this sound like you?....If only a little bit?

Most importantly, if you're quietly cool and sometimes a little geeky, do drop me a line as I'd love to hear from you.

The Traveller Profile

Headline: Dreaming of Summer

Hi!

The most important thing about dating for me is laughing. Lots and lots of laughing! If you can make me laugh then we're half way there. I will of course offer up my side of the comical bargain.

I am always looking to explore new things or ideas.

Travelling has always been part of my life and I relish visiting places far and wide. I love going off the beaten track, and being one of the locals, experiencing the real side of a town, countryside, or little village. I'm a sunny, summery person and love the warmth of the sun on me. Everything seems more positive then.

Having said that I adore London too. I like to keep fit and lead a healthy lifestyle.

I would describe myself as fiercely loyal and I always bring laughter to the dinner table. This is sometimes at my own expense!

I'm looking for a spark more than anything.

You are funny and laid back, don't take yourself too seriously and love a good adventure. If you love travelling that would be huge bonus too.

I keep saying I'd like to make a London bucket list, so someone who is keen to explore London over the Summer with me would be perfect.

What's on your list?

The Nice Guy Profile

Headline: Cheeky chap looking for that someone special.

I'm an outgoing, chilled out kind of a guy and I have a "happy go lucky" outlook on life. I do my best to keep myself healthy and active and I'm always looking to try new things and experiences.

I'm a fun-loving, bubbly person, who is completely genuine with a heart of gold.

I spend my time doing a mix of things - seeing friends, exercising, dining out, visiting new places, going on trips / holidays, walks in the park, a lot of the usual things. I'm looking for someone just as fun and positive as me to share this with.

You are someone who's not afraid to be yourself, laughs a lot and can be stupid at times. You are adventurous, independent, love music and film and most importantly someone who has lots of love to give.

Chemistry is essential and ultimately you can only tell in person, so if we click it'd be good to meet up sooner rather than later.

Email me right now if you'd like to know anything.

That's enough example profiles to give you an idea about what you should be writing. I write new ones every week so I discover something else works particularly well then I'll add it to my website or members area.

Do experiment yourself with what works and what doesn't. You might find that a few little tweaks – perhaps a new ending or new intro can make a huge difference. If you get stuck then do have a look at what your competition is writing and it may give you some new ideas.

Chapter Four : How to Wow them with Gorgeous Photos

There's one Golden Rule when it comes to Online Dating and that's to have a "Fabulous Photo". It's the absolute number one, blindingly obvious, most important thing you really need to get right. But most people get it oh so very wrong!

Your Online Dating profile is an advert to selling an amazing product – you. If you don't have a great photo then nobody will be interested in making a purchase. You could have the best profile in the world but if you don't show the goods then nobody will ever get to see it. It's like trying to post a letter out without a stamp.

I've heard all the excuses. What if someone I know sees me? That doesn't matter as they'd have to be signed up to the same site, doing the same thing as you anyway. Most people don't have any issue with putting photos up on Social Media sites and there's no difference when it comes to Online Dating. Besides, anyone that already knows you has a pretty good idea of what you look like.

Photos are there for a variety of reasons. They are to make you look fun and interesting and this helps make people comfortable with you. If you look like someone worth getting to know and stand out from everyone else then you'll have much more success.

Most people are able to scan lots of photos in just a few seconds, so that's how long you have to make a good impression. You'll probably be doing exactly the same thing – making split second decisions based on whether or not you find them attractive enough. There are so many members on most sites that when you begin you'll be more judgemental than you might normally be if you were meeting face to face.

Your main profile shot (that's the one everyone sees first) should just be a clear shot of your head. Never think of putting on a pair of sunglasses or wearing a hat. This just makes you look like you are either bald or hiding something. I once had a date with a gorgeous girl who seemed to have a fondness for Ray ban sunglasses in all her photos. I convinced myself that she wanted to pull off some sexy Hollywood glamour. When I met her it turned out she was hiding a glass eye. I didn't know where to look.

Don't even think about pressing the search button before your photos are perfect. You only have only one chance to make a first impression and in this chapter I'm going to show you how to make it an amazing one.

The Two Secrets to a Great Photo

There are two very simple things you MUST be doing in your photo. It's so easy that it's surprising how often it's forgotten. Women do it more than men but it works for anyone. The first is to smile! The brain automatically associates positive things to a smile, especially when it's a genuine one. A real smile makes your eyes turn up at the sides and lifts your whole face. This makes you look more approachable and friendly, giving you more chance of making an impact. You might think that mean and moody is better, but if you look remotely threatening you'll be ignored and potentially blocked. Make yourself laugh by thinking of something funny and over exaggerating it. After a few seconds of fake laughing, you'll begin to find it amusing and it can become real. That's because you'll relax and feel happier, releasing positive chemicals into your brain...which in turn make you more likely to laugh genuinely. Give it a try if you don't believe me.

The second secret is to look into the camera and try to connect with the person looking at you. Eye contact is the key to any social interaction as it builds trust. Do your best to look right through the camera.

There's one particular photo that I especially dislike – the Selfie. You'll have seen this shot on every dating or social site you look at as so many people do it. It's especially popular with teenagers who have nowhere to go but their bedroom. Hey, you might even have done it yourself once. It's the one where they take a photo of themselves with a mobile phone....reflecting off a mirror. This almost always comes out at a strange sideways angle too, giving them the rather splendid impression of being both stupid and friendless. Don't do it.

This is sometimes combined with the other contender for "worst photos" – the half-naked portrait. It's become very fashionable for people to send dodgy photos of themselves to potential partners, especially by mobile phone. I'll be covering "sexting" in a chapter later. No, don't start flicking through the book for it, I'm teaching you about photos right now.

You might think having a decent photo is pretty obvious but you'd be amazed by some of the photos I've seen. I've had people in full scuba gear, fancy dress or pink suits of armour. I even remember one chap reading a newspaper on the toilet and quite a few holding giant fish. I bet there are a few "fishy" photographs on every dating site. I know they just want to stand out but it's not appropriate – at least not as a main photo. Your goal is to look like a friendly, sociable and trustworthy partner. Not a clown! People are extremely quick to judge and will make their mind up about you in seconds. I'm not saying you should never try out a slightly different shot. It's fine as long as you have plenty of normal ones. This could serve well as an icebreaker, so make sure it's something worth commenting on.

There's also no point adding too many photos with lots of people around you either. Yes, it might make you look popular but what if it's not obvious which one is you? Even worse, what if someone looking at them fancies them more than you? A single photograph of you hanging out with a small group of people of the opposite sex is acceptable. This acts as what's known as "social proof." In other words, if these people like hanging out with you then there must be something special about you.

It's fine to add a more interesting photo as a secondary picture but it still needs to be clear. Sporty or holiday shots work well for these. It's always good to look like you have an active life.

Don't be tempted to upload hundreds of photos either - this isn't Facebook. Having too many images can work against you as it could be confusing. Some people are so shallow that even if you have nine amazing photos, they'll be put off if the tenth looks even the tiniest bit suspect. Remember that I told you about the psychology of this before. There are many people out there who look for a reason NOT to contact you rather than reasons to get in touch. If they think you might look a bit larger in photo seven, or unhappy in photo three then they'll never get in touch.

If your photo would serve as a good icebreaker then it's worth using it. If it doesn't add any value then don't include it. This means no joke photos of cute kittens, funny sayings or anything you aren't even in. You'd be surprised at the photos dating sites have to reject each day.

I advise you to stick to four photos and these should be:

1) Your main head and shoulders, a smiling photo shot.

2) Another head and shoulders shot with a different expression, background and change of clothes

3) Something that shows your full body

4) An interesting/sporty/amusing photograph or all three if possible.

When other members are looking at your photos and reading your profile they are looking for a way to connect. If you have one that's a little bit unusual then it gives them the chance to comment on it. Perhaps you are visiting a famous place or running a marathon. Don't go over the top and try too hard though. Stand out for the right reasons, not because you look like somebody you'd cross the road to avoid.

What if You Really Don't Want to Add a Photo?

I've never really understood why someone would join a dating site and then choose not to put their photo up. Yet you'll still see thousands and thousands of profiles where you can't see what they look like.

Some people tell me that they don't want people they know seeing they are on there. Yet, they'll happily have a photo up on LinkedIN or Facebook. It makes no sense. If you don't have a photo then people will suspect the worst and assume you are so ugly you aren't worth dating. What are you hiding? I can understand not having a photo if you are in the public eye or a celebrity, but there's no excuse if you aren't.

I have heard good looking people tell me that they want to be judged on personality rather than their looks. That's fine in the real world, but not how it works on online. The absolute bottom line is that if you don't have a photo then you are wasting your time. People are so busy that they will just focus on the profiles with photos and reject the blank ones.

Some sites do let you add a "favourites only" restriction when you upload a photo. This means it's not visible on general searches, but only to the people you decide that you want to be able to see it. It's still a completely pointless option, but it's better than nothing if you really don't want it on display all the time.

It might well be that you don't think you are good looking enough to make it worth adding a photo. If that's you then I'm going to give you some brilliant tips about how to make yourself more photogenic. Remember, having a photo is ten times better than having no photo at all.

Your Main Photo

This is the most important one that everyone will see first so make it count. Get a friend to take a photo of you on a decent camera. Most modern mobile phones have great cameras on them so there's no excuse not to experiment. Ask them to take a few in natural light and pick a good one. Wear something you look great in and remember to smile!

I expect you'll be nervous to start with, so take lots of photographs.

Keep this in mind: **The photo must look like you on a really good day.**

How to look your Best

There are several things you can do to be more photogenic.

-The very first thing is to maintain a regular skin maintenance regime. That's nothing complicated – just remember to wash, exfoliate a few times a week and moisturise every day. I'm not talking to just the women, but you guys too. It's so important if you want to look younger and healthier. Good skin will have less shine, so your photos will naturally look much better. So cleanse, tone, drinks lots of water and get plenty of sleep.

-Ladies, go easy on the make-up but do wear some to ensure you look as beautiful as possible. Guys, don't be afraid of a little concealer if you have dark shadows under your eyes.

-Bright lipstick colours will make you look younger and more outgoing, rather than darker choices.

-Vaseline on your lips will make them look softer and more kissable

-Use a moisturiser that has a least a factor SPF15 to protect your skin from sun damage.

-Eye drops can make your eyes look brighter and some will make your pupils look bigger, a great thing to increase attraction.

-Turn your head to the side slightly and avoid facing directly at the camera. That can be much more flattering if you have a rounder face.

-Copy the celebrities. If you want to slim your arms, put one hand on your hip and point the elbow away from your body.

-Lean in towards the camera if you want to look slimmer. This makes your head look bigger and therefore gives the illusion of a smaller body. (You should watch out for this trick in other people's photos online too as it's commonly used)

-Use your body posture to look more confident. Put your shoulders back and stand up straight. Uncross your arms too.

-The best times to take outdoor photos are in the hour after sunrise and the hour before sunset. These times give the best lighting as long as you make sure the sun is in front of you.

-Use the Flash in moderation. It can often ruin a perfectly good photograph.

-If you are indoors, stand in front of a white wall. Your camera has built in colour balancing settings and this will help it make your face look the right shade.

-Take LOTS of photos, whenever you get the chance. The more you take then the more likely you'll find one that you like. Not even the supermodels look good in every photo, so the more you have to choose from the better. Only you need ever see them and you delete the ones you hate for good.

What to Avoid

Some photographs can do you more harm than good. Don't be tempted to use these type of photos, no matter how amazing you look in them:

1) Airbrushed arty photos. They are easy to spot and you won't have a hazy glow when you turn up for your date in real life.

2) Photos from five years ago. They must be recent (within 18 months) or you won't be recognizable.

3) You and an ex-girlfriend/boyfriend. The more attractive they are then the worse this is. Nobody wants to compete with an ex and it suggests you haven't got over them. It won't help if you crop or black out their faces either as that will make you look crazy as well.

4) Anything with alcohol in. For many people you might look like a fun person if you have a drink in your hand, but to others you are just a party mad alcoholic. Play it safe.

5) Scenic or funny photos that you either don't appear in or are hard to spot. Cute piano playing kittens or you in a crowd during a fun run are just a distraction.

There is some debate about men having topless torso shots and women showing off their bikinis. You might attract the wrong type of people but if you've got it then there's no harm in flaunting what you worked hard for. A six pack or toned body will always get lots of interest but if you don't have these then keep it wrapped up. Make sure you stick to just one of these types of photos and put in your album alongside your more conservative ones. Ask yourself how you'd feel if a prospective employer were to somehow take a look at your images. Would you feel embarrassed or proud?

The Rotation Trick

Here's a very sneaky little tip that can boost your chances. Once you've had a good selection of photographs that you are happy with, don't upload them to a site immediately. Instead, stick to three or four. After a month or so, take off the ones you have and replace them with the ones you have saved.

By doing this it's almost as if you are a whole different person. You'll find that when you search you will start to recognise familiar faces and they almost vanish and don't register in your mind. This is why it's a good idea to shake things up a bit. New photos will get attention and people who have previously dismissed you may give you a second glance. This can work well with a change of username at the same time.

Warning: Don't do this if you are proving successful and things are going well. You don't want the people you are corresponding with to get confused or forget who you are. It's only worth doing this if you've had a break from the site.

Ask Friends

I hate looking at photographs of myself and you might well be the same. This can make it hard to know which ones are better than others. After a while you'll be able to work out which photos are better than others, but to start with you should take some advice. Email a few to some close friends of the opposite sex and ask them which ones they think make you look good. They'll have a much better idea than you will and their suggestions may surprise you.

You can also use your friends to help when you are out and about. Ask them to take a few shots when you are out doing something fun. You don't need to use them but it's good to have some saved up for future use.

Here's another piece of advice when it comes to photographs. When you are searching for possible matches on a dating site, don't dismiss everyone based on their main image. We often scan 1000s of images in a split second, working out who we like the look of and who we don't. Perhaps you have ruled them out because they aren't smiling or because they don't' seem your type. So you won't even get as far as reading their profile to find out if you are a good match or not

The truth is that everyone can look completely different in a variety of photos. They might well have a much better set in their photo album which others will miss. So even if you aren't sure about the first, you should give them a chance and see if you can find a better one. If you do, there might be one that you prefer.

This mistake will cost them lots of possible interest but you'll have more chance of a response if you do contact them.

Tools of the Trade

Photo software has come a long way in the last few years. Online Dating sites are improving the way you upload your photos and some will let you rotate, crop or adjust them. You shouldn't rely on this though, as they aren't that advanced....yet. They are perfectly adequate but you want to make them look as good as possible.

Photoshop is the most common photo editing tool, but it's also very expensive and difficult to learn to use correctly. There are now free photo tools that you can download to your desktop or on your camera phone to make you look like a cover model. Your phone may well come with some great software already built in, but there are wonderful alternatives if you need them.

The best of these are:

Pixlr

Available directly from the website, this is pretty much the best free photo editing software on the planet. It's as simple or complicated as you want it to be and perfect to improve your images. Use it to take away red eye or to sharpen up a background.

Instagram

This is one of the most popular photo apps available to mobile users and is primarily for social media sites. All images will be saved as square shapes but you can apply very distinctive filters to them. For example, you might wish to add a golden haze to give your photo a sunrise feel. Or you can give it a vintage effect for a 1970s look. A small tweak with one of these features can have a huge impact and will make you stand out from everyone else.

Fotor (Fotor.com)

This is so incredibly easy to use and great fun too, so the best choice if you aren't as computer savvy as you'd like.
You can access this either directly on the website or by downloading the free app.

A quick word of warning here : Use these tools to correct minor faults, such as light balancing or adding a border. I don't want you to play around with the images so much that you can't even recognise yourself in them. Use the tools very occasionally to spice up your photos rather than turning them into modern art.

Getting the Professionals In

If you are serious about dating then professional photographs can be a great investment. This doesn't need to be expensive. Have a look on a site such as Gumtree.com and you'll find lots of photographers offering cheap deals. You may even find student photographers who will give you a free shoot in return for building up their portfolios.

Do some research before you hire one and make sure you've seen some example photos. Double check that the price you are have agreed to pay covers the photo shoot, some edits if necessary and the complete right to your photos. There are some companies who will make it appear you are getting a bargain photo shoot which can sometimes include your hair and make-up. The con is that if you ever want to see the results you have to spend a huge amount for the DVD hard copies.

As I said earlier, don't use any photos that look too edited so don't use the "Makeover" photographers. You won't have Vaseline on the lens or photoshop to hide behind when you meet your date in real life.

Chapter Five : Getting Used to the Site (Upping your Game)

OK, so we're up and flying now! You've got a perfect profile, attention grabbing photos and you're sending out irresistible messages. It's time to step things up a gear while I teach you some advance tricks and techniques.

There's no particular order to this section, just lots of really useful tips for you to learn. However, before you start to read any further I want you to take some time to send out your own messages and have a good play around with the site. I don't want you getting overwhelmed with all the powerful stuff I'm about to explain to you.

If you've not sent out at least twenty messages and spent a few days on the site then it's not time for you to read this yet. Come back here once you've done that for me. If you have, then you will have probably got some mixed results but at least you'll know how the site works.

Every site is different, with its own way of doing things. The features and processes will be the same but with perhaps different names. If you are ready, let the games begin.

Learn to Use the Filters

When you run a search you'll see thousands and thousands of possible matches. It's hard to work out who is going to be worth dating and I don't want you to be overwhelmed. To avoid this, have a look at the search filters and have a quick play with them. Think back to your deal breaker list and about the ideal person you want to meet. You can quickly rule out anyone who doesn't fit your criteria.

Be very careful not to limit yourself too much. Are these things really so important you aren't prepared to even have a quick look at their profile? The more filters you put in place then the more opportunities you will miss out on. I had a client who had put in so many ridiculous filters that he only matched with three girls on a site. He couldn't work out why the site was so quiet until I pointed out his error. It is fine to be a little picky but you also have to be realistic.

Adding to Favourites

Almost all sites let you build up a collection of profiles you are keen on by adding them to your "favourites." This can be a useful feature but not the usual way most people use it. That's because most sites will notify the user once you've done this. They do this as it stimulates more views and upgrades. Who wouldn't want to pay just to find out who all these people are that like them so much?

Message them first while you are viewing their profile and add them to favourites once you've starting chatting. That way you can keep track of the ones you are getting on best with. It's easier to look at them there, than trawl through countless messages in your inbox.

When Should you Respond?

I often get asked if you should reply quickly to a message or make them wait a while for your response.

In real life, you wouldn't want to appear too keen but online dating is quite different. You are competing for the attention of someone who is probably also talking to quite a few other people. If you don't reply quickly enough they'll lose interest and talk to one of them instead.

You want to keep the conversation flow as natural as possible. This can be hard if you are having several at once. If you get a reply from them, try to write back within a few minutes. No essays or trying to be too clever as you just won't have time. Strike while the iron is hot.

Life will get in the way and you'll find you both have to go off and do other things, like eating, working and sleeping. If you have to go, then explain politely and get back to them as soon as you get the chance to. When you do return, let them know you were thinking about them and make them feel important.

The smoother the process of getting to know each other, the quicker you'll be able to arrange a date. You'll find that the more times you do this then the easier it will become.

Instant Messaging

If a site has an instant message feature then you can use this instead of direct messaging. It's pretty much the same thing, but it can be a faster way of chatting as there are no other distractions.

The dynamics change as the questions will come much quicker. It's a good chance to be funny and flirty as it's more like a real conversation.

If they ask you to sign off the site and use another instant messaging service (either online or by mobile) then politely decline. You don't want to be sucked into endless chats that drag on for days, weeks, months. People who want to use other messaging services are more than likely doing it just so they can talk to lots of people at once. It's an ego boost and a test to see if you'll do what they ask. Don't do things their way. Tell them that if they want to talk to you then this either needs to be face to face or by phone.

If YOU are talking to several people at once, which I hope you are, then don't bother with the Instant Messenger. It's a fun thing to do every now and again but it can slow down your progress if you have to focus on one at a time. Only use it if the site is quiet or someone has especially caught your eye. Otherwise turn the feature off if you can and stick to plain old emails.

TOP TIP: Try and keep all contact on the site until you are comfortable. When you are ready it's fine to swap numbers, but don't give them too much of your other personal details. You don't want them friend requesting you on Facebook or sending flowers to your office.

The Truth about 'Winks"

Most dating sites have some sort of "Wink" or "Wave" feature. This allows you to signal you like a profile without actually writing a message. You can often do this even if you aren't a paying member.

Women tend to do this as they think they are being coy, showing interest without making the first move. Men do it as a way of contacting lots of women in a short space of time. Both are hoping the other will be intrigued enough to write back. Pressing a wink button is so much quicker than reading profiles and writing messages, so it has to be a good shortcut...doesn't it?

I want you to know that sending winks is mostly a complete waste of your time. If you've been doing this and haven't had much luck then that could be a good indication why it's not working.

Most people will never respond to a wink as it shows absolutely no effort has been made. It can be insulting and looks like you can't be bothered or are too shy to write an actual message. You won't be taken seriously or considered a worthy match as they will wonder what is wrong with you.

It won't work if you have a stand out photograph either as you'll be thought of as a player or timewaster.

Don't be a silly Winker and send them a short introductory message instead. This will have so much more of an impact. Male or female, you need to take control.

There are a few exceptions when it's OK to wink if you really want to:

1) You can wink if the other person has a blank profile with just one boring photo. If they haven't written anything then there's no point trying too hard.

2) You can wink if you want to remind someone they owe you a message. Perhaps you've been corresponding for a while and it has gone quiet. Rather than message again, you could try giving them a gentle nudge with a quick wink.

If you get a wink from someone and want to get to know them it's fine to wink back. This sometimes alerts you both to the fact that you like each other. Hold on a minute though - you still need to send them a message immediately so you can maximise on the attention. I'm not letting you off that easy.

You can try something simple like:

"Thanks for the wink! Looks like the site is telling us we'd be a great match, so let's find out for ourselves. Shall we chat?"

Or a little cheekier:

"Hey, just saw you winked at me. You've got my attention now! So tell me…what did you like about my profile? ;)"

I should also mention that some sites allow you to send an Icebreaker instead of a Wink. This is a specially prewritten message such as "I like your Profile" or "Fancy a chat?" These are determined by the dating site and you can't change them if you aren't a paying member. They are marginally better than winks but it's still MUCH better to write something personalised. Popular profiles will quickly tire of seeing the same Icebreaker messages over and over again.

Who's Online?

Many sites will tell you exactly "Who's Online" when you run a search. This is a wonderfully useful feature that many people overlook. You can use this to your advantage and to give you the edge over your competition.

If someone is showing up as being "online" then you know they are still using the site and you've got more chance of getting a reply. If you contact them while they are online then they'll get your message instantly, giving you the chance of a real time discussion. Your message will be first in their inboxes and top of their profile views as well. The other bonus is that you can usually see when they log out too, so you won't expect a reply for a while.

So when you run your next search, always tick the box to filter it to show only the members online.

Do keep in mind that thanks to smart phones, this information isn't as accurate as it used to be. We can now all log in from our phones rather than desktops, which can mean shorter "active" sign on periods. Members are just logging in to check emails or to distract them while they travel home from work. It's still a good indication that they are actively using the site and they'll probably check in again within a few hours.

The Best Times and Day of the Week to Use a Dating Site

Members log in to dating sites at all times of the day (or night) and on every day of the week. There are certain key times that you will find more active members than others. While it's useful to know these, it's not essential and not something I want you to worry about too much.

I'm including these as I want you to have as much knowledge as possible.

There are three main times that dating sites are busiest:

Morning - Usually around 9am – 10am as members arrive in their office

The first action is to check any emails that arrived overnight and find out if the people they liked have continued the conversation. Some companies ban the use of dating sites during work hours, but it's easy to use a mobile phone to get around this. All the same, messages tend to be at their shortest during these hours.

Lunchtime - 12 – 2pm. This is the peak time during the day as there is more freedom to log on during a lunch break. Guards are still up though as nobody wants to be caught online dating by a colleague or friend.

Evening – 8pm – Midnight. While some people will switch on the computer as soon as they get home, others will want to eat and unwind with some television first. After this they will be much more relaxed and looking for something (or someone) to grab their attention. Nobody else will be watching so they are free to spend more time messaging.

Other times can be busy, such as the commuting hours but these are much more variable.

Friday afternoon is the best time of the week to message when online dating. People are winding down at work, looking forward to the weekend and are looking for a distraction. If they have no plans to go out then they may be more open to a date invitation on the Saturday or Sunday.

If someone is sat at home late on a Friday or Saturday evening you may find they are more likely to respond than other times. They've made the decision to stay in rather than go out so there is a tendency to want to connect with others. Perhaps they have drunk a few beers or cracked open a bottle of wine. That's why I call it the "Flirty Dirty" period – the time they are most likely to let their inhibitions go!

Wednesday and Thursday evenings tend to be the most common for meeting up on real dates. The start of the week is just too early to be going out and weekends are kept free to spend with family, friends or parties. That means that if you want to get a date for later in the week, ask them out on Monday or Tuesday. Nobody wants to appear too keen so you have to give them enough notice.

Location, Location, Location. How Far Should you Cast your Net?

When you first start looking online, keep your options relatively open. Search within the nearest 50 miles rather than trying to only meet your neighbours. If you think about it, 50 miles by car or train isn't that bad if you are in love. It's only 25 miles each if you meet in the middle.

The wider the pool of singles you have then the more chance you have to meet someone. You can give priority to those nearer you by all means, but I don't want you to miss out on opportunities. I wouldn't go above 50 miles though as it can make things more difficult in the long term. If you love travelling or driving then it might not be such an issue. I have a client who often goes on dates hundreds of miles away just because he enjoys the process so much. However, I also know someone who flew from London to Las Vegas to meet someone she'd been chatting with online. The sad thing is that he didn't bother to turn up. She had a fabulous weekend all the same and met some lovely guys when she was there. Sometimes you do have to take a little risk or two.

Chapter Six : First Contact and Magical Messages

In this chapter I'm going to teach you exactly how to make contact with singles to get them intrigued enough to write back. You can easily waste a lot of time if you aren't sure what you are doing and lack of response is the main reason people give up online dating. Writing messages that get replies is so much easier than people think:

You don't need to spend ages reading profiles
You don't need to think long and hard about clever things to say.
You certainly don't need to write long detailed messages
You won't get stuck when you find bland or empty profiles

I'm going to teach you some very powerful stuff but it will only work if you are willing to put a little thought into it. The more you do then the easier it gets. With my strategy you'll soon find you can write about one message every two minutes, or roughly 30 an hour.

How Men and Women Act Differently on Dating Sites

Men and women approach online dating in different ways, and once you realise this you can use it to your advantage. Men tend to collect up their "favourites" and then contact many women at once, in one big hit. This is called the Shotgun approach and is very much hit and miss. They don't care whether the woman is twenty years out of their age group or only interested in certain types – everyone gets included. If the woman does decide to reply to them she won't always realise that she's competing with the twenty others he's written to that day, or even that hour.

The result of this is that popular women can often be inundated with emails from men on the site. They might get so many emails from every Tom, Dick, Harry and Rajan that they won't have time to read them all. It may be easier just to delete the messages before they clog up their inboxes. The good matches will get lost and cleared out with them.

Some women also believe that they should wait for men to message them on dating sites. They might have the old fashioned view that it's up to men to message them first or are worried about appearing to be forward. So they wait and wait and wonder why they never seem to get messages from men they are interested in. This can often be a very long wait indeed and if you do that, you'll only end up being contacted by the guys nobody else would even consider.

The secret is to be proactive and actively target men you are interested in. Don't sit and wait for them to come to you or someone else will snap them up.

Imagine you are applying for a job and your dating profile is your CV. Would you send out your CV to prospective employees or would you expect them to come and find you first?

Men absolutely love it when women message them first. It is very flattering. It's not overly flirtatious to write to a man - after all you are both on a dating site with the same intentions.

Guys, you probably won't get as many messages as female members. That's good as you won't be as distracted and it gives you more time to write carefully crafted emails. If you do things differently from everyone else then you'll be eliminating the competition.

What you Need to Say

The secret that I'm going to share with you is Cheeky, Flirty, Banter. These three things are key to the most dating success and without them you are unlikely to get very far. It's not about being sarcastic, rude or making people feel bad. Instead, it's about making them realise you are the most fascinating and fun person they could hope to meet.

Imagine you are in a bar or at a party. How would you get their attention? Perhaps you'd look over and smile. You need to convey the same emotion in your first email. Make it a little cheeky yet friendly and tease them a little. Type smiley symbols such as: :) and ;) to show that you are joking to make things obvious. Write just enough to get them hooked and capture their imagination. Ask them how their day is going or what they are up to for the weekend. I'll go over this in more detail shortly.

As I promised you before, you don't have to write long essays to get a reply. You'll be contacting lots of people every day, so sending long messages can really zap your energy and motivation. If they are popular they won't have time to read everything anyway, so short messages will get their attention. Three or four lines is plenty , providing you say something fun, interesting and different that shows you are a good match. For example you can joke about something they have written, ask a question or comment on one of their photos. I've included some example messages that have worked for my clients at the end of this chapter.

Needless to say, everyone has different tastes and they won't all reply. This could simply be because they aren't a paying member, they are exploring other options or you remind them of an ex. It's a real numbers game and even if they aren't interested you could make someone's day by paying them a compliment. Once you start to get good at this you can probably expect at least a 20% reply rate. When you consider the average person only gets about 2 to 3% that's a huge improvement.

Time Saving Tip: Learning to Scan

You honestly don't need to read every single word of their profile...at least not straight away. You are going to be looking at hundreds of different people which can be time consuming if you aren't careful. It's possible to quickly scan a profile and still understand what type of person they are and what they are looking for. Have a look at the key areas and find something you either have in common or that you can comment on. Check for any reasons that you might not be compatible too as it's important you only contact good matches. You can read the full details of their profile once you've started talking.

How to Handle a Blank Profile

As you'll remember back from the previous chapter I wrote about on writing a profile, you'll know how important it is to have conversation starters in your text. Quite often you'll come across bland, dull profiles that are don't say anything at all. They'll be vague or full of generic "I like going out for a few drinks or staying at home with a DVD" type statements. Even worse, they might be completely blank which makes it impossible to comment or find similar interests.

If they have a selection of photos you could use these as an icebreaker, but if there's no text at all then there is a good chance they've only just signed up. This makes it a fantastic time to contact them as they won't be getting many other emails…yet.

Don't waste time writing to them though as chances are they will be unable to read the messages if they aren't paying. These profiles are the only time it's acceptable just to use the Wink or Wave feature. If they can't be bothered to write anything then why should you? If you get a positive response then it's worth sending a message like the one I'm about to share with you. This is because finding out who winks/likes you is usually only a premium feature and indicates they are able to reply if they wish. Keep in mind that just because they winked back doesn't mean they'll respond to a message, but it's certainly worth a try.

Try sending something along the lines of this:

Hi, thanks for the wink!
I was just about to send you a clever witty introduction, talking about the things we have in common and why we need to meet. But your profile is blank! So tell me everything I need to know about you?

You might also get a notification that someone has added you to their favourites list. If they haven't contacted you within two hours then it's fine for you to make the first move and reach out. Send them a message like this:

"I just noticed you adding me to your favourites. Were you waiting for me to make the first move? Cool :) Hi, I'm XXX. What's your name? x "

Warning! Copy and Pasting – the Lazy Dater's Quickest Route to Failure

Some people cut corners and try to avoid putting any effort in when they first join an online dating site. All that profile writing, searching and emailing can be very time consuming if you aren't seeing any results. So to save time, instead they'll bang out a quick two line message to anyone that takes their fancy, being sure to include their phone number or email address in the message.

Let's try and see this in a different scenario. You are in a busy bar, looking to find a hot date. Would you really just rush around the room, handing out bits of paper with your phone number on them?

What do you think the success rate is of this strategy?

The secret is to engage with each person individually, flirt with them, make them feel special and build up trust. Only then can you exchange numbers. It's the same formula you need to stick to when it comes to dating online. If you just send a phone number and no personal message it will be deleted and you'll be forever classed as a weirdo.

When it comes to messaging, you'll get out of it what you put in and you need to put some effort in to get the dates you want. The difference is that you'll get the results so much quicker if you do it properly from the start!

The Beginning: Get Them to Open Your Email

Some people get lots of emails so it's important to make sure yours stands out from the rest. That way you know it will be read first.

So what do you need to do to catch their attention? It's simple really. Take a look at their user name and if they've used their real name then make a note of it.

Then all you need to do is put this in the subject line.

When they go to their inbox and see it looking like this, which email do you think they will open first?

Hey

Hi

Hello

Hi Suzy!

Hello there

Good day

It's human nature to feel a "connection" if you see your name written down. It makes you want to open it quickly to see if they actually know you. By doing so you've helped form a subconscious bond before you've even started talking.

Of course, not everyone will use their real name so you can't always do this. However, they'll sometimes sign off with their real first name at the end of their profile too, so play close attention to that.

Give it a try and see if you notice a difference.

The End - Signing Off

Now I've shown you how to start your message, it's just as important that you know how to end it.

Just like your profile, you need to end with a question or an invitation. Otherwise, you are just making some statements that don't require an answer or reply. Treat it exactly like a conversation you'd have if you were standing opposite them. If you forget to do this then there's no reason to reply.

Finally, add your real first name and put a kiss (x) symbol next to it. This is a dating site so it's appropriate and not too forward. If you feel uncomfortable doing this then by all means don't worry about the kiss, but it's a nice touch. When you use your real name then you are showing them that you are willing to be open and honest. It makes you seem more like a real person so they won't be able to ignore you as easily as someone who leaves this out.

How to Guarantee your Profile is Always at the Top of Searches

The higher up in the dating site search results you are then the quicker you'll be found. This means it's much more likely you'll be contacted than those who are several pages down. There's a great way to make sure that you are always in the top few listings. Check back on the site a few times each day and log out again once you are finished. By doing so, you'll be listed first in the searches as one of the most recent members to log in.

Some sites will let you pay extra to be top of the searches but this isn't something you should do. If you are seen to be top of every search every time a user logs in then it's pretty obvious you've paid up. This may look a little bit desperate and is best avoided.

Winning Email Templates

Here are some simple templates you can use NOW that take all the guesswork out of composing an email. They are all adaptable so you can change them to fit the profile you are contacting. Once you start using them try to think up some of your own. The very best messages are the ones that come from your own mind and heart.

1) Hey, nice profile – you sound fun. You like cooking then? What would you make to impress me on a first date? Get it right and I might have to show you my own culinary skills!

2) How come most of your photos have you holding a drink? ;)

Ok....what's your favourite cocktail? If it's one of my top three I'll take you out for the best chocolate martini you've ever had. Deal?

3) So tell me... apart from taking selfies, what's your biggest talent? ;)

4) I like your profile, how's your weekend going? Tell me, do you pout in real life as well as in your pictures? ;)

5) I've got a challenge for you: If you beat me in a race I'll buy you dinner...but if I beat you then you have to take me for cocktails. Deal?

6) Loved the profile...But what do I have to do to make you smile? ;)

7) My friend and I have a bet on about you. Can you help?

She thinks you have hair extensions but I reckon you are all natural. Who wins?

8) I'm stunned. I can't believe that you love staying at home with a DVD or going out for a few drinks. Guess what? Me too! You'll be telling me you are equally comfortable wearing a ball gown or a tracksuit next. Then we'd REALLY have something in common ;)

I think we are made for each other...let's talk!

9) Hey,

You have a lovely smile but you don't say anything in your profile.

This makes it REALLY tough to write a clever witty message that will get you interested. So...I'm going to have to guess!

Am I right in saying ...   (Then write something along the lines of one of these)

Most of the time you are positive and cheerful, but there has been a time in the past when you were very upset?

You are mostly shy and quiet, but when the mood strikes you, you can easily become the centre of attention?

You have a great sense of humour

You have a large collection of My Little Ponies

How did I do?

10) *Wow - that's an amazing trick! Your eyes (or hair) change colour in different photos. How do you do that?*

I can work my own magic – I bet I can make your face turn red ;) x

11) *Bonjour   What's "Fancy a drink sometime" in French? ;)   (If they have a foreign name or say they are from a different country)*

12) *You probably have the cutest smile I've seen on here....I'd kick myself if I didn't say hello :)   So how was your day?   x*

13) *What do you teach your kids? How to be as cheeky as you? (If they are a teacher)*

14) I'm intrigued by you... but I have been warned off Spanish looking men - apparently they are all crazy ;) What's your number? Let's talk.

Getting Too Many Emails?

I really want to make you aware of some strange behaviour you may come across. It seems that some people get lots of interest and get loads of emails......only to never reply to them!

What I'd really like you to do is at least reply to more of these people, even if it's to say "thanks but no thanks." It's just plain old courtesy. To make this easy for you most dating sites even have standard responses such as "thanks but I'm not looking at the moment" or "You aren't my type." It only takes a few seconds and they'll at least know that you have acknowledged their existence.

Some people don't reply because they don't want to have to pay for the service which is quite strange. If you aren't serious about meeting someone then why fill out your profile in the first place? If you start making the effort and communicating with people then you'll soon start making new friends and lining up dates. If you want to learn to swim you have to start by putting your toe in the water after all!

If you really aren't interested in making contact with anyone or are perhaps currently dating then it might be a better idea to hide your profile.

My dating clients often tell me that they find it hard to make time for online dating in their busy lives. They work all day and are too tired in the evenings to do anything proactive.

As a Dating Expert, I can see how it might seem time consuming. It takes a while to search for people you like the look of, compose witty messages and keep the banter going.

But it really doesn't have to be. The object of the game is to get their attention quickly and then arrange a meeting while the interest is there. You don't have to write long essays back and forth for weeks. The first message only needs to be a few lines long – just enough to get them intrigued. After a couple of replies, speak on the phone for ten minutes and then arrange your first date. Endless messages only build up unrealistic expectations and prevent you from ever meeting up.

Here's a quick tip which will help you find time for dating….Turn off your television! It's the biggest time waster there is and its main function is a "partner replacement." Most people spend all their time either staring at it or looking forward to seeing it again.

Believe it or not, studies have shown that watching too much television can actually triple your urge for material things. Just think how many adverts you watch, consciously and unconsciously. On top of this, it's been shown that every hour of your day you watch makes you 5% unhappier!

You only need to spend about 20 minutes a day to make online dating work. If you knew it would guarantee some fantastic dates, would you be able to find time to do it then? Picture the end result before you start and you'll soon be able to fit it into your busy lifestyle.

Second Chances

You've contacted lots of people you like on the site but haven't heard back from some of them. You don't want to hassle them so most people simply give up at this point. But I'd strongly advise you to give it another go.

Keep in mind that people lead busy lives and might be inundated. This means they accidentally overlook certain emails or they plan to open them but end up getting distracted and forgetting all about it. Resending your email to these people almost guarantees an increased open rate. Perhaps they are seeing someone else right now or are away on holiday.

No, you don't have to bombard them with a succession of more and more frustrated emails. I've seen this go badly wrong as the messages get more and more desperate. "Not sure if you've got this" leads to "Why do you think you are too good for me?" which can lead to "You're so rude, I hope you stay single for the rest of your life" Subtlety and politeness are the only way forward. Here are a few tips to see if you get better results

You know this, but always write proper, personalised messages. If they feel you've made an effort they'll be much more likely to reply.

Wait at least three days before you contact them again. They might well have not had a chance to log on the site, especially over the weekend.

Change the Subject Line. If you do this it will look like two different emails. If they've not read the actual message then they won't even know they are the same.

Make it clear you are resending it. Say something like

"I'd hate you to miss this" or *"I'm resending this as I know we're a fantastic match."*

If you still don't get a reply this time, then don't send any other messages. You've made your point and they've made theirs. They know you are interested so you're much better off contacting others instead. There's always the chance that you might hear from them at some point in the future, but not if they think you are harassing them.

The Games People Play

In the process of working out who is worth dating and who isn't, you'll come across many people who will try and test you. Finding the right partner is vital, so it's important to weed out the time wasters and bad matches. They'll ask questions or make strange statements, just to see how you react. If you get it wrong you'll probably never hear from them again, so it's not worth taking the risk. You aren't going to play their games as YOU are the one who must be challenging instead. The very act of showing them you aren't like everyone else will make you seem like much more of a catch.

By way of an example, I once had an email from a girl who I could tell was trying to work me out. I got the impression she was used to men begging her for dates, so much so that she toyed with them for her amusement instead. She told me that she was looking for someone to 'entertain her'. So I just gave her the website address for a kids party magician who twisted balloons into weird and wonderful shapes. This made it clear to her that I was worth pursuing and lead to several interesting dates where she confessed what she'd been up to.

The more online dating that you do then the more tests you'll come across. These won't rattle or confuse you after a while. It's much easier to completely ignore the loaded questions if you don't want to answer them. Ask them your own question instead or make a jokey reply.

A common strategy is to try and catch you out on something they might be suspicious about. They may suspect you aren't being honest with them about a certain issue – usually your age, job or if you are really single. They'll ask the same questions over and over, in different ways to see if you give the same answers. As long as you are being completely honest (or have a good memory) then this will never be a problem for you.

I'd better warn you now that a lot of people have absolutely no intention of ever meeting anyone. They are just bored and enjoy chatting away to anyone who is remotely interesting. It's simply an ego boost for them to get them through their day. Some of these can be converted into dates, but they'll probably be chatting to so many other people it's almost impossible to hold their attention. It's almost an addiction for them and they need their fix. If they won't meet you after a week or so of messages then cut your losses and give up.

Chapter Seven : How to Get a Date

You're doing really well now and are quickly learning how to generate interest from your online dating profile. I'm proud of you but you have more work to do!

Your goal is to get lots of dates, not just lots of interest. So sooner rather than later you're going to have to step away from your computer and start meeting real people. This means you have to both arrange a date and one of you has to be the one to suggest it. There are two ways that this will happen: Either by messaging on the site or over the phone. Each has its own advantages and disadvantages:

Asking for a Date by Computer

Pros: Quick and Easy, with less chance of rejection.

Cons: You don't know each other well enough so there's more chance of one of you flaking at the last minute. Are they really the person they say they are?

How to do it: If you are going down this route then you need to spend some time getting to know each other. I've seen some people suggest a date in a first message, but that's never going to work. Nobody is going to agree to a date after just one or even a couple of messages, so you have to put a little effort in. Not too much but spend just enough time to get them interested and sure they are worth dating. Banter back and forth and then test the waters. These two messages can work well:

"I'm not really a fan of typing away at a computer forever. Much better to get on with it and see how we get on! What do you think?"

OR

"I've got to head out now and I don't use this site very much…..BUT I'd love to get to know you some more. What steps can we can take to make that happen?"

They should take the hint with either of these messages and they may even suggest a time for a date themselves. There's also a good chance they will suggest speaking on the phone first and give you their number. If so, the next section will be an extremely useful way of progressing things.

Asking for a Date by Phone

Pros: You get an instant answer and you can get it booked in and confirmed straight way. You'll also get the chance to build up the rapport, so there is less chance of them cancelling.

Cons: It can be scary to speak on the phone for the first time and it can be easy to spoil things if you mess up.

How to do it: It's much easier to get someone's mobile number than you probably realise. You have to do it in the right way that leaves them feeling comfortable. In order to get their number, you'll have to do some messaging back and forth first. After a few questions have been answered and asked by both of you, you can try being direct. The message template I'm about to give you has been proven to work in less than three minutes, providing you remember to Intrigue, Tease and Build Trust as I've shown you before. There's no need to make a big deal out of your request so ask in as natural a "matter of fact" polite way you can. Go with a message that's a bit like this:

"I have to rush off now, but I Would love to get to know you some more - why don't you give me your number and I'll give you a call this evening?"

It really is a simple as that. What's the worst that can happen? If they are keen they will agree but if they are unsure they'll make an excuse to delay it. You can pick up again a little later and ask once more.

The phone may fill you with dread but it's definitely the best way to guarantee a successful date. Many people absolutely hate using a phone as we are so used to typing away anonymously. I'm going to teach you how to make the phone your best friend rather than something you are terrified of. Before we do that, we need to make sure you are ready to make that call and sound like someone worth getting to know.

Sounds Good

Your voice is one of your most important weapons for increasing your attractiveness. But are you using it to your advantage?

Our voices are something we all take for granted and therefore we don't give them much thought. But you really need to be aware of how you sound. Do you sound passionate, interesting and fun or scared, boring and incoherent?

I've known people to get lots of interest via online dating but then completely blow it when they start speaking on the telephone. That's only because of nerves and you can learn to improve them. If you can learn to speak well then it's useful every day of your life. Not only can you use it to get a date but to ensure a job interview goes well. Here is how you should go about this:

1) Record your voice and play it back. Most mobile phones will have a facility to do this if you can't do it from your computer. Many people are surprised as to what they sound like as we hear things differently to the way other people do. This is all because of the way sound echoes and resonates in your head.

2) Pay attention to the way you sound. Are you speaking too softly, loudly, fast or mumbling? The slower and clearer you speak then the better you'll come across. Successful people always leave people hanging on their next word.

3) Copy someone you know. This can be a film star, politician or a TV personality. Find someone that you know members of the opposite sex find attractive. If you aren't sure just ask a friend. Pick someone like George Clooney or Kiera Knightley. When you've worked out who you want to sound like then listen to them as much as you can. Do they talk slowly or quickly? What makes them so special? Take what you like and discard the rest.

4) Perfect it! Pick up a newspaper or a book and practice reading it out loud. Try to do it slowly and make it interesting. Imagine you are reading to someone you are attracted to. Paint pictures with your words and you'll soon be able to do this naturally.

5) Use it. Once you've mastered the technique then use it at every opportunity you get. This can be on the phone to sales people, in supermarkets or anytime you want to stand out.

The First Phone Call

Once you've learned how to speak, you'll be able to have amazing conversations. If they aren't face to face then they'll be on your personal dating tool – your telephone. It can be incredibly exciting having your first call as it breathes life into someone you've probably only chatted to "virtually." You'll both be a little nervous but that's absolutely to be expected. Here is what you need to do in order to make sure they don't hang up before you've arranged to hook up.

Firstly, arrange the call for a time when you know you'll be alone. This will be in a quiet place, with no distractions or anyone listening in to put you off. Take a few deep breaths and then call them. Or if they are ringing you, breathe and then answer. Either way, do this on time and don't keep them waiting. If you don't answer they might not give you a second chance.

1) The telephone forces you to lose one of your most powerful senses – eye contact. The other person can't see you nodding your approval or shaking your head so you need to make up for this. Instead say things like "I hear you" and "I agree" and they'll know you are both in sync.

2) Keep the first conversation short. I always suggest you limit your first chat to ten minutes. Use it mainly just to establish a first date. I'll explain more about that shortly. If you spend two hours chatting away before you've even met, what will you talk about when you finally do meet? Once you've met up, feel free to speak as long as you want, but for now ten minutes is enough.

3) Treat the call as if you are auditioning. Imagine they are sat opposite you and overact! Even though they can't see you, if you gesture when you speak it will make you sound more engaging. I find that standing up helps you sound your best as it's easier to breathe.

4) Most importantly – smile! Try saying this line out loud now - "I'm having a wonderful day." Say it three times, once with no expression, once with a big grin and once with frown. Do you see how smiling can lift your mood and makes you sound so much

friendlier? A smile comes through when you talk on the phone and it's taught to anyone learning how to be better at telesales.

5) Work the answerphone. This tip is valid for when you leave a message as well as your own voicemail recording. The last thing you want is for somebody to be turned off just because of your ten second message. Keep it simple, warm and friendly. No gimmicks, no sound effect and no jokes. Smile when you record it and keep it short and sincere. If they were supposed to answer, don't think you are off the hook and you can get away with asking them by voicemail. There's nothing sexy or romantic about that. I just want you to say something along the lines of:

"Hi! It's (name) and I'm just calling as we planned. Call me back once you get this as I'm waiting to speak to you!"

Asking the Big Question

I expect you may now be wondering who should ask who out on a date. Should you take charge or is it better to wait for them to suggest it first? The strategy here is slightly different depending on whether you are male or female.

Men: It's usually better for you to do the inviting. That's just the way it's been since cavemen times. Let them know you've loved chatting and it would be great to meet face to face. Tell them where and when you'll be waiting, don't ask where they'd like to meet. You will of course have been paying attention to everything they've said, so you'll know the sort of thing they would like to do.

This will earn you serious brownie points too. If they aren't keen on your suggestion then they will offer a counter proposal.

Women: While it's the man's job to ask you out, you have to let him know it is fine to do so. Put him at ease and drop hints or gentle suggestions. Make him aware that you are free on Sunday or that there is a new art exhibition you'd love to visit. Only be direct if he's clueless and won't take the hint!

What to Say if you Can't Get them to Agree to a Date

You want endless love, not endless chat. Talking and never meeting is one of the biggest mistakes people make with online dating. Life is just too short for this!
You find someone you like through online dating and send a few messages back and forth. You're both getting on well so you suggest that you speak on the phone or meet up. However, rather than agree, you get this reply:

"Thanks, but I like to take my time to get to know someone.   Let's just speak on here for now"

This is something that I notice quite a lot and it can be incredibly annoying as well as confusing. Everyone will of course want to take things at their own pace, but you do have to be realistic. You are on a dating site so it's only fair to expect people to go out on actual dates!

If you are one of these people who is just a little nervous about dating then that's absolutely fine. You just need to take a little risk and get yourself out there. You won't meet anyone hiding behind a computer and you won't really know if you are a good match until you meet them.

There's little point writing endless messages back and forth as the other person will soon lose interest. Why would they spend all that time and effort on you if you aren't ready to give anything back? They'll just move on to someone else who is happy to see them.

You don't want to be begging someone to meet you, so if you ask twice and they refuse then cut off the discussion. They may well realise what they are missing and agree to see you but if they don't you've lost nothing.

The Joy of Text

Your phone isn't good for just speaking alone, but for texting too. Texts are a great way to keep in touch quickly and keep your conversations going. Please don't use this as a substitute for actually talking though. Oh – and it's probably not a good idea to ask them out by text either. It may work but if you've not built up the rapport they will probably try to cancel at the last minute...by text of course.

Use texts to flirt and build momentum in between dates and to remind them that you exist. If you've got their number then you shouldn't be messaging through a website anymore. You've passed through that stage and it would be a step back. Texting is your best option, in moderation. There's nothing worse than being bombarded all day long so a little goes a long way. Every now and again you can send them something amusing to let them know you are thinking about them. This can just be a question about something you've discussed or a comment that you hope will make them laugh. This could be as simple as:

"Hey you, how is your day going? x"

That's fine, but it's a very dull question and not something that will kick start their imagination. It's much better to go with a question/statement that will make them more likely to respond.

Go with something they told you, to show you were paying attention. Such as:

"How did your meeting with your boss go? Hope it went well x

Or mention a shared joke:

"I just saw that mad bunny advert on TV and thought of you. Made me smile. Have you seen it? x"

Flattery always works well:

"Hey you. I've got to buy my brother a birthday present. You have good taste. Any ideas?x "

Or go with something completely random and bizarre, to get them thinking.

Do put a kiss (x) on the end of your text messages to show you are romantically interested in them. If they put more than one, you don't have to match it and add the same. One will do, at least until you are in a relationship. If you get to that stage then do feel free to put as many kisses on the end as you please!

This brings me on to texting timing in general. Should you reply back instantly or make them wait a while? There are various opinions on this. Some experts will tell you that it's best not to appear too keen and to delay your response so they think you are busy. Others will say you should reply immediately while the interest is there. I'm going to tell you that you should mix things up a little bit, depending on how serious you are. If you really like them and have some free time, then reply back quickly. If you are busy and not that sure then reply when it suits you. This doesn't mean keeping them waiting for hours as that's rude, but it's fine to leave it an hour or two. The exception to this is when you are confirming or being asked to confirm a date. Get back to them as soon as you can so you can iron out the finer details. If you keep them in suspense you'll give them the impression that you aren't that bothered. Be respectful and expect the same back.

One of the problems with text conversation is knowing when to finish. After some light chat, you might want to go off and do something else. You'll need to end the conversation but the other person might not be ready to drop it. The result is that you end up chatting complete nonsense and ultimately losing interest. To avoid this happening, it's much better just to be honest and tell them you have things to get on with. They should accept this and give you some space.

Sexting

If you've not already heard of sexting you are going to be in for a bit of an eye-opener. Sexting is the wonderful combination of two very powerful things - sex and texting. I'm telling you about this now as it can be a natural progression from regular texting or when you start using dating apps. You've got the phone in your hand and it can be tempting to get flirty.

Sexting can take several forms. The simplest of these is a variation of good old phone sex. Rather than speaking on the telephone you can type your fantasies and instantly text them to the other person. This can be especially popular to those on the shy side. If you want to do this it's always best to test the water first, just to make sure that the person is really ready for them. If you misjudge the mood you can easily end up scaring them away thinking you are just a bit of a pervert. So take it slowly, building up the sexual tension and build the momentum with each message. Think of it as a striptease. You want to aim to do it slowly and meaningfully, rather than going rushing to the end straightaway. Instant gratification spoils all the fun.

This will work best when you know they are alone. If you think for just one second that they are becoming uncomfortable then stop immediately. If you blow your chances it's going to be very difficult to get things back to how they were. By taking it one step at a time it's so much easier to backtrack a little and then move forward again a little later.

If the thought of this is getting you jittery then you might want to skip this next section. Go make yourself a nice cup of tea and join me in the next chapter. Still there? I thought you probably would be. I'm now going to talk about advanced sexting. Yes, it gets more complicated than just simple text messages. Almost all mobile phones nowadays have a camera on them which can be used to send naked photographs back and forth. Don't pretend you've never taken or thought about taking a few saucy snaps yourself! We both know you aren't as innocent as you look.

There is another dangerous side to this that I want to quickly mention. The scary thing is that many teenage girls feel huge pressure to take photographs of themselves and send it to boys they are interested in. Unfortunately, boys being boys, more often than not will send these photos to their friends. Their friends will of course pass these on to their own friends, usually pretending the images are of their own girlfriend. This means that one secret photograph can end up being seen by hundreds if not thousands of people in an extremely short space of time. You've only got to look at certain pages on the Internet to see how popular this picture sharing really is. No, I can't recommend any in particular, you'll just have to trust me on this one.

It's so easy to take a few saucy pictures and assume that they will be kept private. That unfortunately is not always the reality. Just look at how many celebrities get caught out doing this. There is probably a story about it in today's newspaper. If there isn't then I can almost guarantee that some famous person is sweating profusely at the thought of making tomorrow's headlines themselves.

If you do this properly and have absolute trust in each other this can be a great way of getting to know each other, especially in the early stages of dating. Just treat it like you would with anything else in life and don't do anything you would be embarrassed for your friends and family to see. Do you really want to send nude photos to a complete stranger? What would happen if things don't work out between you? Did you honestly trust them to delete the photographs? If things end badly what would you do with any messages or images on your phone?

If you aren't absolutely certain that these photographs will be between the two of you, be very very careful. You can still send flirty texts and photos back and forth, just keep it toned down and preferably fully clothed. It's usually best to leave things to the imagination as fantasies are often much more long lasting than revealing everything too quickly

Camera phones are not something to be feared at all. They can be a wonderful way of reminding each other that you are thinking of them. If you know that they are having a tough day then why not send them a smiling photo to cheer them up. If you've not seen each other for a while or are far apart, send a well-timed photo to bring you closer together.

How to Prepare for an Amazing Date

Dating should be a fun, exciting experience full of opportunity. However, for many people it can be extremely scary and fill them with dread. Some admit they are worried the other person will reject them. Or they fear that they might embarrass themselves during the date.

You are going to be doing lots of dating, so to end this chapter I want to show you how you can mentally prepare yourself and get rid of your dating anxiety.

Make a Mental Movie. Rather than focus on what might go wrong, you should be thinking about all the things that may go right. Sit down somewhere quiet and play a short film in your mind about the evening from start to finish. Picture everything going fantastically well with you both laughing, flirting and having fun. This mental rehearsal helps everything go smoothly.

Questions. Communication is the secret weapon for a successful date, so make sure you give some thought about what you'll be talking about. This will stop you getting tongue tied and ensure you don't have awkward silences. Read up on the latest news stories and think about topics that may interest them. Perhaps they would rather discuss popular television shows or tell you about their ambitions. Be ready with some fun questions to get them to open up.

Cheer up. You can trick yourself into feeling happy and positive. To do this, look into a mirror and hold your biggest smile for at least two minutes. If you find it difficult, place a pen between your teeth. Smiling releases the chemical serotonin so you feel better and less stressed and your brain can't tell it's a fake smile. Try it!

Use nerves to your advantage. Remember that they are probably just as nervous as you. It's just a surge of adrenaline which the body produces to keep you on your toes, giving you the "butterflies in your tummy" sensation. A few nerves are nothing to worry about and they are usually a good indication you are doing the right thing. After all, if you didn't care then why bother turning up? It's only by putting yourself in testing situations that you will be able to have exciting new experiences. Congratulate yourself on facing your fears and growing as a person.

Do your research. If you prepare in advance, you'll feel so much more relaxed. Work out exactly how you are going to get to your date location and what you'll be doing. That way you shouldn't get delayed or have to make difficult decisions when you get there. So do have a sneaky peak at the menu online if you are going to a restaurant or locate some happy hour venues if you are doing drinks.

Project the future. Once you get to know someone better then you'll obviously feel more relaxed. A good technique is to pretend you've already been dating a while. They are no longer a stranger, but someone you know well. This will instantly make you feel more relaxed and optimistic.

Be open minded. Don't go into your date with the expectation that you're going to fall in love and run off together into the sunset. That just puts unnecessary pressure on yourself. Instead, enjoy the process of getting to know each other. If you don't fancy them then at least you will have a lovely evening and you never know who they can introduce you to or what you can learn from them.

That's just about all you need to know BEFORE you go out on a date. The next chapter will be all about HAVING amazing dates!

Chapter Eight : Meeting Up: How to Have the Perfect First Date

You've put in all the hard work so you've now got the most fun bit to look forward to – the actual date! This is where you move from online dating to real world meetings. Online dating can help you get to know each other before you meet, but it's only a face to face environment that can test your chemistry.

Before we start planning, I want to quickly go over some safety advice. It's just a precaution but I'm not letting you out the door until you've read them. They apply to both men and women so I want everyone to read them:

Safety First

It's always important to remember to be careful. While most people have good intentions, you have to look out for the few that aren't. Here are a few common sense tips that I want you to stick to. Say them over and over again until you know them backwards.

1) Before you meet, let someone else know where you are and who you are with.

2) Always meet in a public place with other people around. (Don't let them pick you up from your house, no matter how flashy their car is.)

3) Remember to have your mobile phone on you at all times, fully charged of course.

4) Don't give out personal info such as your home address or where you work, or accept them on Facebook until you get to know the other person better.

5) Never leave your drink unattended or accept a drink from a stranger without watching it being poured.

6) Don't get drunk. You need to keep control of everything.

7) Trust your instincts. If something feels wrong then leave.

8) If you decide to take things further, always make sure you do it safely!

9) Follow-up after a date. Make sure the other person got home without any problems even if you don't want to see them again.

10) Don't be afraid to question the other person's motives. Make sure this is in line with what you want.

The Dating Guru Rules

I'm expecting you to do a lot of dating over the coming months, so I'm going to set some ground rules to make sure you don't get bored, overwhelmed or frustrated. You aren't going to fancy every single person you meet so don't waste your valuable time on the wrong people. I learned these rules the hard way so you don't have to make the mistakes I made. They might sound a little brutal, but our mutual goal is to find you the partner of your dreams.

Rule One: Set a Time Limit of just 90 Minutes for your First Date

There are several reasons why this is a great idea. Firstly, the last thing I want is for you to be stuck with someone you can't stand for any longer than you have to. Secondly, if you do enjoy their company then this will whet their appetite and make them long to see you again to develop things further.

You'll need to think up some excuse as to why you can't spend too much time with them. It doesn't need to be a real reason but it should be a believable one. I'll leave it up to you but it's best to go with something along the lines of being really busy at work or other social plans. You don't need to go into too much detail as you won't owe them any sort of explanation. There's no need to apologise either as you are going to let them know they are very important to you. Despite your hectic diary you are able to make time for them anyway.

At some point one of you is going to suggest meeting up. This will either be by email or phone and you'll need to say something like this:

"I'd love to meet you but I'm so busy at the moment. I've got lots of work on/ a sick kitten/ early starts etc. Rather than delay meeting how about we just have a short date after work or one lunchtime to see how we get on?"

The clock starts ticking from the agreed date time, even if they are a bit late. I know you won't intentionally be late as you know how rude that is, but if an earthquake hits you can start timing from the minute you sit down. I don't want you staring at your watch constantly as your focus should be on the other person. When the time is up, tell them you enjoyed meeting them but really do need to head off. They may well try their best to convince you to have one more drink, but don't get suckered into that. One more drink quickly becomes three more drinks and before you know it you've missed the last train home.

You're probably about to ask me if you should still leave even if you are having the most wonderful date of your life. If you really are then I'll let you extend it by another 30 minutes or so…but no more! It's brilliant that you've enjoyed yourselves but leave the date on a high with you both wanting more. You can always arrange to meet again in a few days for a longer period of time. If you suddenly admit that you aren't as busy as you suggested they will suspect you might lie to them about other things – not the way you want to leave it. Stick to your original plan, see them again soon and go home happy.

If you turn up for a date and they are nothing like they said they would be, don't feel obliged to last the 90 minute duration either. If they are rude, dirty, twenty years older than their photo or something doesn't feel right then you have every right to leave. You don't owe them anything and your time is better spent travelling back than wasting any more time on them. If there is nothing wrong with them but they are just not your type, then it's polite to stay though. They have made the effort to meet you so try and be friendly. It's only a short period of time and you'll probably have fun. Besides, you don't know if they might have a friend who would be a better match. There's really no need to burn bridges.

Rule Two: Mix Things Up a Little

If every date you have follows the same structure then they are quickly going to seem like Groundhog Day. The most common dates involve going for drinks, a meal or to see a film. There's nothing wrong with these but remember your mission is to get to know each other. Films and Shows won't allow you to talk and meals can be awkward. Coffee shops are much better places to date than bars as they are cheaper, quieter and less busy. Every high street has countless places to grab a coffee so you'll always find somewhere.

Sometimes just going for a walk can make a great date or have a look round a new area. Whatever you do, try and think out of the box to make it more exciting and fun. If you aren't arranging it then go along with their plan, but make a point of spicing things up for a second date.

Rule Three: No Sex on a First Date

I'm not here to lecture you, but please do take things slowly when it comes to jumping into bed. Without a little build up and romance, it's just a casual romp which can lead to regret. Sex should be the icing on the dating cake and something you both think about over time. If you do it too quickly then they might think you sleep with everyone which is a turn off. It's pretty judgemental and hypocritical I know, but it's unfortunately how many people think. Everyone is different and I want you to take things at the speed you are comfortable with. Three or four dates is about average.

Rule Four: Don't Spend Too Much

Dating can be really expensive, especially for men. If you are going out all the time the costs can soon add up.

You really don't have to spend lots to impress someone. If they expect it they are just money grabbing anyway! However, you need to make it look like you've made an effort. I'd suggest you take a look at some of the great deals you can get on the new "offers" websites like Groupon. You'll be able to book amazing restaurants and experiences at a fraction of the price. For example, I've seen cocktail parties and three course dinners with drinks for less than a third of the normal price. Keep your eyes open and you'll find plenty of bargains. The best thing is that they need never know how cheap it really was if you are subtle about it. Whipping out a voucher is never sexy, no matter how big the saving and they will think you are a cheapskate. It's better to produce that when they aren't looking or pretend you've gone to the toilet.

Women have their own expense for dates too, which many men don't even think about. This might be a new outfit or getting your hair done specially. Again, this isn't really necessary as most men won't know the difference anyway!

Rule Five: Relax

If you get too nervous or worked up then you can ruin the start of a wonderful relationship. The secret is to just relax and go with the flow. You aren't there to be interrogated and you certainly don't have to answer any questions you don't want to.

Some dates will be good, some not so much, but each one will teach you a few new things. Treat every date as a mini adventure and go in expecting to have fun rather than assuming the worst. If something does go wrong or you say something embarrassing then you can both laugh about it. Try to see the funny side of the situation and then quickly move the conversation on to something else.

My Good Dating Cheat Sheet

If you want to have a great date, then here are the key points to keep in mind. You might want to copy these down and keep them on you to refer back to.

Be kind and considerate. Observe good manners and treat your date as you'd wish to be treated yourself.

Be generous. For the best outcome, men should always offer to pay but women should not take advantage of this and over the period of several dates they should take their turn.

Take an interest, make sure you are a good listener. People love it when you pay attention to them and they'll instinctively like you a lot more.

Use Body Language to your advantage – be flirty, smile and pay attention to the signals they are giving off too.

Be honest about your intentions and don't play games. Follow up afterwards, even if you aren't interested.

Do something around an activity, so the focus isn't just on you. Make sure it's something where you can both still talk and get to know each other.

Dress up and take pride in your appearance. Brush your hair, floss your teeth and make sure you smell nice. Remember you want to present the best version of yourself possible so do make the effort.

Don't talk about exes or competition with your dates. Focus on making them feel special instead.

Have several talking points pre-prepared. This will make you seem interesting and helps fill any awkward silences.

Pay a compliment to your date, but don't go overboard or you'll sound insincere.

How Men and Women Think Differently when it comes to Dating

In the never ending quest to find true love, we all get to experience a variety of first dates. No two first dates are the same and not all of them will lead to a second. While both sexes put effort (so it's hoped) in to the date, each one thinks about it in a completely different way.

Once on the date, each sex has all sorts of things going through their mind. Thoughts can race from everything that could do with picking the right place, to future life together, to whether or not the date will end with a kiss or perhaps something more.

A woman's mind races on a date. It's as though the inner monologue is on a hamster wheel and doesn't seem to want to get off:

"Does he like my outfit? What about my hair? I wonder what his mother is like? What if she still does his laundry? What if she lives with him? Oh no, what if he would want me to live with them. What did he say his last name was? I don't know if that will work well with my first name. What about our kids? Does he even want kids? I didn't catch his profession. Did he say it? Maybe he doesn't have one and that's why he lives with his mother."

Women are multi-taskers by nature. Thinking about multiple things allows a woman to gauge her surroundings, her date and her feelings all at one time. Women think from a point of view of finding someone to take home to their parents. Someone who they can buy a house with and have children. They think from their heart.

Men, on the other hand, generally tend to focus on one thing on a date: the woman. There is no other way to put this and no other way is necessary. Men just think about what is in front of them, which is their date. Most men are euphoric at the fact that this girl in front of them said yes to a date at all.

Men also have a tendency to think of the more practical aspects of the date since they know that the man has to take charge. Atmosphere, conversation and ensuring that his date is comfortable are all important. They also know they must pick up the bill at the end of the date.

This is not to say that women are looking at a date from a more selfish perspective, as they can focus on things that will eventually matter in the long run.

Both parties eventually think, on their own, as to how a date will end. Each sets different standards in their own mind as to what should happen after the date. The best thing in this regard is to not force anything. An awkward ending to a great date can be a killer.

After all, neither sex truly goes on a date just for the fun of it. We all want the same goal…. that much anticipated request for a second date!

How to Flirt

Flirting to get what you want is natural human behaviour. By being playful and showing interest then you make the other person feel wanted and therefore more accommodating. Flirting can boost morale and make the world a happier place….if you do it correctly.

It is human nature to flirt when we find someone attractive, but surprisingly many of us flirt with people we don't fancy, just for the sake of it! Whether it's to gain approval from others, for a confidence boost after a particular messy break up or just to while away the dreary hours at work, nearly all of us have been guilty of compulsive flirting. This often stems back to childhood, when babies flirt naturally for survival. They flirt to get attention and to be looked after and this can continue into adulthood. Grownups can often flirt to manipulate, get their own way or to make sure they get what they want.

Here are some of the things you can do to make sure you flirt more. When you are flirtier then you'll instantly become sexier and more attractive too. Try these techniques in shops or when you are negotiating as well as during dates.

1) The most important thing you can do is to hold eye contact. Long lingering looks coupled with a cheeky smile will show you are interested in them. If you do this properly they will find it hard to say no if you ask for something as they won't want to lose your attention.

2) Mirroring is a fantastic way to build rapport and make them like you. This means that you copy what they do. If they scratch their nose, wait a few seconds then scratch yours. If they are opposite you and raise their right hand, then raise yours. The reason this works is because people like people who are like themselves. If you are doing what they are doing then they'll put you on the same level as themselves. Just keep it very subtle or they will realise what you are up to.

3) Point at yourself every now and again when you use positive words. They will then subconsciously connect you with these words. For example, tell them what a fantastic weekend you had and how you had a perfect day off.

4) Talk to them about their interests and make them feel special about them. Tell them how wonderful and fascinating you find these things and how it makes them stand out from everyone else. Pay attention to even the smallest of details and they'll be amazed when you bring them up in conversation at a later time. If you don't know much about these hobbies then do a little secret research on the internet and you'll impress them even more.

5) When you ask for something, nod your head as if you are saying "yes." This will subconsciously increase your chances of getting a positive reaction.

6) Recent studies show that the very action of holding a warm drink can make people assume you are a warmer person. A cold drink can have the opposite effect. That's another reason why coffee shop dates can be very effective.

How to Tell if they are Interested

If you aren't sure if they are in to you or not then pay attention to their body language. They will be giving off signals all the time that you can read once you become aware of what to look for.

When you first meet someone, watch to see if they raise their eyebrows quickly. When we see someone attractive, we unconsciously raise our eyebrows at them for a split second and this shows you have noticed them.

Where are their hands and feet pointing? If they like you then they'll be pointing right at you. Even if they seem happy, if they want to leave then their feet will be pointing away from you, getting ready to escape!

The eyes can give away a person's true feelings. If their eyes are dilated (big and black pupils) then it can indicate interest. Also, if they are looking at your eyes and then down to your lips a lot (the flirting triangle) they could be keen to have a little kiss.

Are they laughing at your jokes? If they are giggling at everything you say, no matter how silly, then they might well be attracted to you. People only really flirt genuinely when they are happy and comfortable.

Do remember that it's always best to look for several signs before assuming attraction. If you can see lots of indications that they are interested then you are probably on to a winner. Be sure to keep an eye out! All in all, a bit of mild flirtation never hurt anyone, so sit back and enjoy it while it lasts!

The Friends Zone

You never want to end up here. It's game over when they tell you that they only see you as a friend, not a partner. It's very easy to get stuck in the friend's zone if you don't make your interest clear.

This is what you need to do to signal your intentions:

1) Flirt, flirt, flirt. You need to try and escalate things physically. Stay clear of anything creepy of course, but you do have to lightly touch them every now and again. This can be as simple as touching their arm or giving them a quick hug at the start of the date. Once you are sure they are comfortable, step it up a little. Perhaps you can give them a high five or hold their wrist while you pretend to be interested in her watch.

2) Be a Man. Women need to respect your masculinity if they want to date you. This means paying the bills, being confident and not chasing them round like a lovesick puppy.

3) Be a Woman. Ladies, play up your feminine side. This means laughing at his jokes and allowing him the chance to look after you.

3) Be Romantic. If you want them to feel romantic towards you then you need to set the scene. Take them to romantic places, buy them small gifts and treat them like they are the most important person you've ever met. If they feel special then you'll be making them feel good too – meaning they want to spend more time with you.

4) Make your interest clear. How will they know you like them if you are too nervous to tell them? Bite the bullet and make your move. If you delay they'll assume you only want to be friends and it's very hard to turn it round.

5) Remember all is not lost. Many friendships do eventually turn into relationships and can often be longer lasting because of it.

How to Spot a Liar

Being able to tell when someone is lying is a very useful skill, whether it's in dating, business or in your general day-to-day life.

However, it's easy to get it wrong if you don't know how to do it properly. Of course, everyone tells the odd fib from time to time but these are mostly tiny white lies. When getting to know someone, you will want to be able to tell if they are married, generally just making things up as they go along, or further down the line knowing whether they might be cheating on you. So I'm teaching you this so you can avoid any potential misunderstandings or even heartbreak.

Here are some tips on how to get the bigger picture and spot the giveaways:

1) Watch the eyes. Liars will often use prolonged eye contact or try to avoid looking at you at all.

2) Listen out for what they say. If they are constantly saying things like "To tell you the truth", "To be honest..." or "No word of a lie" then they are usually doing the opposite.

3) Look to see how rigid their body is as the stiffer they are then the more chance they are lying. They might not wish to give any clues away so will fold their arms, cross their legs and freeze like a statue.

4) Everyone has a "tell" which is a slight nervous reaction to something. This could be something as simple as brushing the hair out of their eyes, a little giggle or a sniff. The idea is to note how often they do it, and if it's frequent it might well be covering up deceit. We all scratch our noses or shuffle our feet, so don't be too quick to judge!

5) Liars will try and hide the palms of their hands, so be cautious if they have their hands behind their backs, under the table or grasped together tightly.

6) Liars will play with objects in their possession such as a glass, watch, mobile phone or hair. They may also put an obstruction between themselves and the other person, often something as simple as a coffee cup. This is a subconscious way of attempting to 'barricade' themselves to relieve the tension of lying.

7) Adrenaline rushes through the body when people are fibbing, which can mean they blink a lot more and their eyes dilate.

8) According to research, true "enjoyment smiles" are so big and bright that you'll notice a crinkle around the eyes. These authentic smiles last for less than five seconds. The "masking smile," or lie smile, tends to last longer than five seconds, doesn't involve the eyes, has a hint of negative emotion, and may be crooked. If they are a slightly more mature person then there's always the chance it could be Botox.

9) Watch out for their facial expressions and see if they match what they are saying, as expressions are hard to hide. For example, are they saying they are excited and happy, but their face is unsmiling and serious?

10) It's all in the details. Liars will tend to overcomplicate their stories and specify every little detail.

They do this so they won't be asked too many questions after. Listen out for exact timings and place names that most people would gloss over.

The same rules apply for spotting lies as for flirting – you need to look for several indicators rather than just one. A person might fold their arms because they are cold rather than being defensive so you can't read too much into one gesture. If they fold their arms, avoid eye contact and keep looking down at their shoes then things become much clearer.

Top Tip: A kiss on the cheek is the perfect way to start a first date. It sets the scene right from the start. After all, it's a date, not just friends meeting up or a business meeting. A playful kiss at the end makes it clear that you are both interested in each other and keen to meet again. Don't just rush in – build up the tension and make sure they are comfortable. If you find they are leaning in to you and keep looking at your lips then there's a good chance they want you to kiss them

Be on Time

It's acceptable to be five minutes late but any more than that is unfair. It makes them think you weren't really bothered about meeting and that they aren't important to you. Your chances could be ruined before you even see them. If you know that your time keeping isn't great then put the extra effort in to get ready a little earlier.

Most people are reasonable and understanding but nobody likes to be taken advantage of. Phone batteries do die and trains do get stuck in tunnels. If an emergency happens then do your best to ring or text your date immediately to let them know. Tell them you are really sorry and will be there as soon as you can. Most will be fine with that as long as they are aware of what's going on. If they don't know where you are then they will assume you are standing them up which is soul destroying and embarrassing.

If you are more than ten minutes late then you need to buy the first drink as an apology. Don't even question it and start your date with a long excuse. Telling them how bad your journey was or how your hair straighteners caught fire will not make the first impression any better. Apologise….Joke about it….Get the Drinks In….Move On. That's all you need to do.

If anyone keeps you waiting for more than 30 minutes without an explanation then give up and leave. You can be happy knowing that you never had to deal with someone who had the potential to mess you around and make you feel bad. Never contact them again unless they have a genuine mind blowing excuse. Even then, it's their job to convince you they are worthy of another chance. Make them come to the area you live in this time, but obviously not to your house.

How to Escape a Terrible Date

You've been preparing for hours, stressing over what you are going to wear, and excessively wondering how your date is going to be. You've felt a great connection with them and you've even spoken to them a few times to double check they are normal. The big moment comes when you turn up at the venue, bursting with excitement about finally meeting your date. But the moment you come through the door and spot them, you feel that gut instinct in your stomach that things aren't going to go well. You dart your eyes around quickly, considering in one last hopeful move that there must be some way to escape.

While I would encourage you to do your best, life is really too short to waste it on awful dates. If they have clearly lied to you about their age, hair or size then you have a right to want to leave. Luckily, there are many graceful ways to end a date for the times when you really want to get out. My sneaky tips and tricks are easy enough to use and you won't need to feel overly bad about them either.

Lost and Not Found

If you're lucky enough to go to a big concert or an event with a large crowd, then you can take advantage of the situation to get lost. Literally, lose yourself amid all of the people. While you should invoke this method at the onset of the event, for politeness sake, after about forty minutes, say you're going to the restroom or to get a drink and claim that you simply lost your way back and how stressed you felt. If your date is intelligent enough though, they'll understand the truth and not ask you what happened.

Let's Get Married

Well, if you aren't enjoying your date and things are a disaster, you might as well amuse yourself if you don't have the bravery to high-tail it out of there. The best way to cheer yourself up is to play the "what do you think about marriage" or "are you considering children one day" cards. These kind of questions are the quickest way to get rid of your date by scaring them off. You won't have to deal with crushing guilt, if that kind of feeling gets to you.

Work Emergency

One of the best excuses to use these days that most people will understand is the "something came up at work" excuse. This kind of lie most likely isn't a flat out lie, since most people usually do have work to do outside of the office. Therefore, if you are looking for a pretty realistic excuse, then this is the best option there is. Just have a friend give you a call and then claim it was your boss. Your date will most likely believe your excuse.

Just Be Honest

If you're one of those individuals that believes in being blunt, then simple honesty may just be the best choice. You won't need to feel guilty, you'll get to the point, and your date will understand. It also may just be the case that your date felt just as bad about how things were going. Therefore, this is an amicable way to resolve a bad date.

It's always worth getting a friend to call you one hour into a date anyway. That way you can let them know you are safe and happy…or use it as a way to escape. Perhaps your flat mate has lost their keys and urgently needs you home. Or your imaginary cat has been run over.

What You Need to Do Next

What to do if you do want to see them again, and if you don't.

a) You want to see them again

Brilliant – this is the perfect scenario. Let them know you thought it went well and you'd like to see them again. Assuming they liked you too, they'll be pleased to have their minds put at rest. Make sure you arrange a second date around one week after your first one. Any later and you'll forget the connection, any sooner and you might burn out too quickly! It can be hard to find things to say if nothing new has happened in the time you've been apart, so leave it just long enough for them to miss you.

Hi (First Name) I had a lovely time today and it was great to meet you. We had such a lot to talk about ! Let's meet again soon, perhaps next Tuesday? Enjoy the rest of your weekend. (Your Name) x

Or

"Hey (First Name) I had such fun getting to know you. Let's do it again. Drinks next week? (Your Name) x

b) You don't want to see them again

Perhaps you knew they weren't the one for you right from the first hello. Or things went wrong when they blew their nose on the tablecloth or told you they thought you'd be better looking. If it's a definite no then thank them for meeting you and wish them good luck. I'd advise letting them know this quickly so they don't hold out hope of further dates and start hassling you.

I'll make this easier by giving you some pre-written "Thanks but no Thanks" text messages you can use.

"Hi, thanks for a great evening. We aren't quite right for each other but it was lovely to meet you"

Or you could try:

"Lovely to meet you - it was fun. I don't want to take this further (as we live too far apart/ too big an age difference/ you remind me of my sister /we don't have much in common or whatever you think fits) Good luck and I'm sure your Mr (or Miss) Right is out there!

If they are really keen then they might be persistent and try to change your mind. If this happens, delete their number and don't respond again. They'll soon get the message when they don't get a message. You've been polite and respectful.

Don't give them false hope or kiss/sleep with them if you don't want to see them again. I know that can happen if alcohol temporarily clouds your judgement. Being strung along can bring out the dark side of anyone and they could prove hard to get rid of!

If things have progressed a little too quickly or you've been on quite a few dates, a text isn't the way to break things off. I'm afraid you are going to have to pick up the phone or tell them face to face. I know it's not something you'll look forward to but it has to be done. They've invested time getting to know you.

c) You aren't sure either way.

You aren't necessarily going to fall in love with someone the first time you meet them. Nobody is ever really themselves on a first date, but you should have a good indication of their personality and interests. Part of these may be great, but others may make you a bit more hesitant. That's perfectly normal. If you aren't sure then there's absolutely no harm in going on a second date with them. If you do, think about what else you'd like to learn about them beforehand.

The Art of Multi Dating

This may amaze you, but I want you to be dating lots of people at the same time. At least until things get serious with one particular person. That's because I never want you to be waiting around for someone to get back to you, staring at your phone and wondering why they haven't replied. You should never put your life on hold, so keep your options open.

It's a natural reaction to get excited about meeting someone for a date. You wonder if perhaps they are the one, so start to think about how things might be together. You don't want to lead anyone on so you cut off all contact on your dating site. If you talk to anyone else you'll feel like you are cheating on your new potential partner. You may even decide to be honest and tell people on there that you aren't looking anymore. Then what happens is you meet, don't feel a spark and are left with nothing to fall back on. Don't burn your bridges!

You may find yourself in the situation where you have had a few dates with someone but you aren't sure where it's heading. You are keeping active on the site and sending out messages. Then you get an angry call asking you why on earth you are still on the site when you are supposed to be dating them.

If you've not agreed that you are officially an "item" and haven't slept with them, then you've done absolutely nothing wrong. There is no need to apologise or lie to them. Let them know you are still dating other people, but tell them how much you like them. This will be your best opportunity to find out how interested they are in you and if it's time to make things more serious.

If you have had the "conversation" or have had sex, then you're going to have to come up with another story. You could tell them that you had logged in to work out how to delete your profile. Or that you wanted to send a polite rejection to someone you had a few dates with before them.

Dealing with Rejection

Everyone has different tastes and we are all attracted to different things. Some like younger, some like older. Some like blondes, others prefer brunettes. If we were all exactly the same then life would be very boring. That's why we should never take rejection personally. I'm a sensitive person so I'm fully aware that's easier send than done. Getting rejected is never pleasant and it hurts! You'll wonder what's wrong with you or what you could have done differently. You'll be disappointed that all your hopes and dreams of a future together have suddenly vanished, which leads to your confusion and resentment. You'll understandably want answers. Unfortunately, even if you can get them to discuss their reasons, it's doubtful they will want to tell you the truth. Nobody likes to hurt anyone's feelings.

You're going to end up doing more than your fair share of rejecting too, so you're going to have to toughen up. When you do it, you'll do it with respect and in the kindest way possible. If you do that you'll never feel guilty about it.

The Ghost Date: The Online Dating Phenomena

Before I end this chapter I want to warn you about something very spooky. There's a strange dating phenomenon that you'll come across quite a bit. You'll go out on a date or two and everything will be going well, then suddenly the emails, texts and phone calls stop. They seem to have completely vanished, never to be seen again. You try your best to contact them but you don't ever hear anything back. Where have they gone you wonder? Maybe they've lost their phone, caught a terrible cold or been abducted by aliens. You'll spend hours going over the possibilities about why they've disappeared. This will also happen all the time with online dating. You'll start chatting and look forward to getting to know them – when they cut you off cold. I call these "Ghost" dates. Sometimes you'll find that you can't even access their online profile anymore. Have they blocked you or closed their account you'll wonder?

The truth is that there are endless reasons why they've gone, perhaps they have got back with their ex, or circumstances have changed. Just maybe they will call you soon, as phones DO get lost and stolen, people do go away with work, they do get ill, and all manner of crazy things can happen in people's lives, but 99 times out of 100 there's one major factor that causes this. Brace yourself, the reality can be hard to come to terms with....They just aren't interested!

Sadly, you'll probably never know the true reason why. My advice is just to accept it and move on. You'll meet lots of these "Ghost" dates along the way, appearing and disappearing seemingly at random. Don't take it personally, but look at the good things you've learnt from the experience. Like looking for a job, looking for "the one" requires slightly thick skin and a realistic attitude. Get straight back on the dating site and start arranging lots of other dates with new people, so you are never in the position where you have to keep waiting to hear back from one person. Lead an active, busy life and you won't have time to worry about these things. Perhaps one day a UFO will land and bring them all back!

Chapter Nine : The Dark Side of Online Dating: Scammers, Conmen and Catfish

Online dating is such a lucrative cash generating business. Where there is money, there are criminals out to claim their own share...and they are getting cleverer than ever. These evil people prey on the lonely and vulnerable and can ruin lives.

It's not just individuals, but whole teams working to rip you off. There are also some so called reputable websites that could leave you heartbroken and with an empty bank account. In this chapter I'll show you the most popular scams. I'll teach you how the conmen work, why they are so effective and how to avoid them. I really don't want this to become a "Scammers Handbook" so I can't tell you absolutely everything the industry knows. If I did then the bad guys would know how to avoid being caught.

Please remember that the vast majority of people are absolutely genuine. I want you to have your guard up so you know what to look for, but don't let it stop you meeting the good ones. It's better for you to be armed with this knowledge rather than becoming a target.

The Fake Profile Scam

I once heard a dating site owner refer to the process of getting the most amount of money dishonestly from a customer as the "Dark

Arts." In recent years there have been a number of scams exposed that have been run by the businesses themselves.

1) Teams of employees were paid to set up fake profiles and use them to make contact with new people who hadn't yet paid. This was to give them the impression they were popular and that they were going to get lots of dates. The flood of interest would quickly dry up once they'd upgraded. One of the biggest clues that all was not as it seemed was that these teams would also send messages to completely blank profiles. A real dater would never waste time writing to someone with no photos or text.

2) Some sites legally run fake profiles by using the "purely entertainment" get out clause. For example marital affair dating site Ashley Madison states in their terms and conditions that:

"Our Site and our Service also is geared to provide you with amusement and entertainment. You agree that some of the features of our Site and our Service are intended to provide entertainment to our users."

I know of some sites that even have set scripts that they use to encourage conversations. They hardly ever deviate from them as it requires too much effort, so you will find yourself getting the same replies over and over. You think that you are talking to gorgeous men and women but in reality they are probably just a spotty teenager sitting in a call centre playing up to your fantasy. Is that really how you want to waste your time or money?

3) False claims. All sites claim to have the most amount of members or have the most amount of successful matches. But how many really publish their results? You can have millions of members but if they are inactive, a site with a few hundred live members can be better. Run a search to see how many are actually online in your area and you'll have a much clearer perspective on whether it's a good site or not.

4) A few sites buy in databases of members in bulk and create profiles for them without these people even being aware. The companies who sell these often swap around details so they can't be traced. The photographs are usually completely different from the person who really wrote the profile so it's harder to trace them.

5) Hiding last logged on dates. The site might look like it's very busy, but it's not always obvious how many are active and when they last used the site. In some cases it could have been months or even years ago as there's no easy way to find out. To make matters worse, you can't usually tell who is a paying member and therefore more likely to respond to your email.

The online dating industry is definitely changing and most sites are now doing their best to clean up their acts. Not everyone wants to play by the rules, so that's another reason to do your research before you try one you've never heard of. The worst sites are just getting sneakier and trying new ways to cheat the system, but they are few and far between.

Some may consider the whole concept of repeat billing to be a scam, but as long as this is made absolutely clear when you join then it's definitely not. If it's just hidden in the small print or in the terms and conditions then it's probably done to rip you off.

The Catfish Scam – Are you Being Baited?

This particular scam has had lots of exposure thanks to the television show "Catfish" which coined the name for it. Put simply, it is people pretending to be someone else.

It's wonderful that more people are much more aware of how this works and to look out for the warning signals. The downside is that this makes it easier for the Scammers to know how to avoid being caught.

The Catfish scam isn't usually about making money, but it can sometimes lead to this. Instead, it's usually about trying to get to know someone who they don't think would normally be interested in talking to them. They set up a completely fake profile using stolen photos of someone else – usually those of a hot model they've found on the internet. These photos are so utterly gorgeous it would be very difficult not to be interested in getting to know them.

A Catfish can be a man or a woman and quite often they are the same sex as the person they are targeting. On rare occasions, it could be someone you actually know in the real world who has a reason to hide behind someone else. They could have a crush on you but are afraid to let you know. Or perhaps they have a grudge or are seeking revenge.

Once they have got your attention, it can be extremely addictive for them and it's hard to stop the charade. It becomes a huge challenge and they will have to lie and keep in character to keep up the pretence. Some Catfish like to talk to several people at once, often using different identities.

The longer you talk then the harder it will be for them to admit the truth. They'll convince themselves that they aren't doing any harm as it's their personality – just with a different face. You'll naturally want to meet up with them for a date but it's an impossible request. They can never see you as the truth would be instantly revealed, so they'll make excuse after excuse to avoid a face to face meeting.

Sometimes they will go to drastic lengths to break off the relationship without telling you the truth. I had my own "Catfish" several years ago who claimed to be an American actress. We'd planned to meet but then suddenly her "sister" instant messaged me from her account to say she'd been killed in a car crash. I didn't believe this for a second as it made no sense. Her sister would not know who I was or be using her messenger. It's quite a sick thing to have done but she probably thought it was her only way out.

Anyone can create an online dating or social media profile in minutes. If they get caught then they can just delete it and set up another almost immediately. If they get banned from the site then they'll try another one or sign up from another location or email address.

It's worth mentioning that completely genuine good looking people are active on these sites too. Just because they have a nice photo doesn't mean they are out to rip you off. I once met up with a girl who claimed to be a supermodel with the photos to match. There was no way she could possibly be the person in the photographs. I met her for a drink, assuming she wouldn't turn up and was stunned to discover it really was her. She'd signed up to the site as nobody ever hit on her unless they were drunk – they were just too scared. The lesson here is that gorgeous people are just as lonely and desperate for love as everyone else.

The Nigerian Romance Scam

Despite the dating industry's best efforts, scammers are still managing to get through the increasing amount of security checks. The worst are based in countries such as Nigeria, using stolen credit cards to purchase memberships.

They set up fake profiles, usually using stolen photographs which are written in such a way that they appear genuine and actively dating. Quite often they just copy and paste someone else's profile text with a few tweaks.

They will then use these profiles to contact, often using special software, hundreds of people each day. While the vast majority will smell a rat, it only takes one out of every few thousand people to fall for the con. The average return on this makes it well worth the scammer's time and effort.

This is an example of the type of poor quality, badly written nonsense email they will send you:

"Your profile is appealing. My name is Tom. I adore and admired everything in your profile. I am really much impressed about your profile and your personalities. You definitely got your appearance so attracting and appealing. I really hope we can get to know more about each other better since we all don't know what the future holds for each of us, besides, communication is the key to a successful relationship. Relationship is not a matter of age differences or the distance. Do not think of the age or distance between us. I would have written more about myself and my photos but can only do that through email. contact me through my private email here lets see where the roads of fate can lead us. ???????@gmail.com. I would be glad to get to know more about you better and if you really want to get to know more about me, get

back to me through my email ??????@gmail.com. Hope to hear from soonest"

They will usually target the most vulnerable people on the sites – the over 50s who have come out of a long term relationship. They can be desperate to connect with someone and feel loved. So the criminals will sweet talk them and make them feel special and the most important person in the world. The conversations can go on for weeks or even months, during which time both sides may confess to being in love with each other. They will share secrets and discuss plans for the future. The Scammer might even send gifts such as flowers or chocolates as a way to build up their trust.

Sooner or later they will ask for a small amount of money. Perhaps they want to come and meet them but don't have enough for a passport. Or they need to pay their internet bill as their wages haven't come through yet. This is just a test to see how deeply they have suckered them in. If they get this money then they know it will be easy to ask for larger and larger amounts. If they realise their plan isn't working they simply disappear and move on to the next person.

If they do get this payment then the Scam steps up a gear. They'll go on asking for more and more money for increasingly outrageous things. Their mother needs an operation or they want investment to launch their own business. They've got the passport but now they need a plane ticket. They've got the plane tickets but are being blackmailed by officials if they want to leave the country.

They've paid the fine but now they need a visa for their pet that they absolutely must bring with them. Now the dog is ill and needs to see a vet. As soon as this gets sorted you can be together at last, they'll promise. They'll beg, cry and tug the heart strings so much that it becomes impossible to say no. The requests never stop until the target runs out of money or patience – whichever comes first.

The most successful of these frauds are perpetrated by teams. One will be responsible for creating the profile, another for sending the messages and another for sending the gifts. You aren't just talking to one imaginary person but several of them. To make this worse, they have people all over the world who are now able to make phone calls to rope people in further. They will have local accents and a good line in conversation.

Some of these scammers are stupid and quite easy to spot but the good ones are learning to keep up with the times. I've heard cases recently of scammers emailing or phoning up dating sites, protesting they are real and trying to discover why they were suspended. Once they learn the reason they know not to make that mistake again.

There are certain clues that they use in their dating profiles which you can watch out for. These include using the phrase "God Fearing" and saying "Am" rather than "I am." They'll write that distance and age doesn't matter too. The men might look much younger in their photos than they say they are on the profile. Many will say they are widows in order to get maximum sympathy. They may tell you that they are a soldier serving overseas so watch out for photographs in military uniform. This is all done to try and build your trust.

The Russian Romance Scam

This scam is a variation of the Romance Scam, but the targets are mostly men. Age isn't so important to them in this case, but again it starts with a fake profile on a website or by spam email. The profiles are almost always scantily clad young ladies and the photographs reflect this.

Some may wait for you to contact them first and then they'll quickly ask you to contact them privately away from the website. They do this as there's much less chance of them being caught or found out. Once they have your email address it goes on to a database of "suckers" and can be sold on to other scammers. So you may end up getting random emails like this one, which claim to be girls writing to you from the official website. They purposely use odd language in order to make them seem more innocent and endearing:

"Hello Dear,
I came across your profile at (xxxxx) I will be delighted to have good relationship with you and to know much better. My name is Rose Glory, I am single and never married. I will wait for your reply. You can contact me at this my email address (xxx) and I will

send you my picture and more about myself. Waiting to hear from you. Please don't forget to contact me direct to my Email address (xxxx) Waiting to read your message at my email box. Rose x "

Ultimately, the scammers are just after your money and they'll begin the same routine as the Romance Scam. They'll do everything they can to convince you to send them your hard earned money in return for what you hope is the chance of a relationship.

The interesting part of this scam is that the photos are often completely genuine and you won't find them anywhere else on the internet. That's because they are taken in professional studios with real models. They are paid to do this in return for using their images. If a potential target gets suspicious then they may ask for a certain photo to prove they are real. They'll ask them to take a photo holding a bible or in a certain place wearing a certain outfit. As the teams have these girls on standby it's all too easy for them to arrange this. I've even heard of cases where these girls also appear on webcam or speak on the telephone.

The Romance Scam is now so advanced that they are able to produce all manner of fake documents in order to convince you. Just because you've seen flight tickets or a birth certificate doesn't mean they are necessarily real.

The Already Taken Scam

Some people are so bored with their marriages (or relationships) that they get tempted to look online for better options. Part of this may just be an ego boost to confirm they are still attractive or because they fancy a quick flirt.

They won't always use their real photos, for fear of being caught, but strangely quite a few do. If you confront them then they'll tell you they have split up or don't talk anymore. It's very hard to prove otherwise.

It's not unheard of for one person to be in a real relationship with multiple partners who are unaware of each other. They try to manage them all at once because they enjoy the attention and love the thrill of nobody knowing what they are up to. Even worse, some do it purely to try and cheat these lonely singles out of as much money as possible. It's just a question of building up trust, asking for cash and then disappearing forever.

The Webcam Scam

This one is hot off the press and so new you've probably not heard of it. It's very simple but also a great money-spinner for the conmen. It's run from all over the world and probably in your own area too.

You think you are talking to someone you have met through an online dating site. You'll chat away and things start getting a little bit steamy. They'll suggest you take things up a level and chat on a webcam. Once you do then their goal is to persuade you to get naughty and do things you would never normally dream of. Hey, it's just the two of you and nobody else can see. So what's the harm?

The cold hard reality hits home the next day when you receive an email that makes you feel sick to the stomach. Not only have they recorded your video session, but they will show it to everyone you know if you don't pay them lots of money. They'll tell you that they have hacked your email address book and most people are so scared they'll pay up. They'll be too embarrassed to even report the blackmail threat to the police.

If you do find yourself in this situation then I strongly advise you never to pay. They are just after your money and aren't really interested in going to the effort of sending it out to anyone. They probably haven't even recorded it anyway. If you do send them money then they will never stop trying to squeeze more out of you. If you are genuinely concerned they have then please do go to the police. If the scammers think you've done that they'll leave you alone as it's not worth the risk.

The Reformed Scammer Scam

There is one last Scam I want to tell you about. This is where a Scammer has been confronted and they have admitted everything. However, it doesn't end there. They will tell you that yes, they were initially trying to con you but during the process they have genuinely fallen in love with you. They are very sorry and want to make it up to you. Slowly but surely they will work their way back into the trust of the victims. After a short period of time they'll dream up new ways to extract money from these poor people once again.

How to Identify if Someone is Genuine

Once you know how, it's reasonably quick to spot the Scammers and Catfish.

It might seem strange, but some Scammers actually use the word Scammers in their profile. They may write "No Scammers" or "Scammers Go Away." This is done to alert other criminals that it's a fake profile and to keep their distance.

-Talk to them on the Phone or even better, by Skype. With Skype you'll be able to see it's really them and at least with a phone call you'll be able to identify their accent. If they tell you they don't have a phone or that it's broken then question why that would be.

-Ask for their full name and do some research on them. Are they on LinkedIn, Facebook? Do they show up anywhere? If so, reach out to them on there too to make sure it's really them.

-If they do have a Social Media account, examine it very closely. It's very easy to set up Facebook profiles in an attempt to look legitimate. However, there are usually plenty of giveaways. Take note of how many friends they have and how long they've had the profile for. If they aren't regularly interactive and posting updates then it's likely it's a dummy profile. Do their friends look genuine or could they be fake profiles too?

-Look at their photo albums carefully. Do any backgrounds set off alarm bells? If they are on a Social Media site then see how many photos are on there too. Are any friends tagged in?

-Copy the photo and run it through a reverse image website such as the fantastic one provided by Google:

http://www.google.com/insidesearch/features/images/searchbyimage.html

If it appears anywhere else on the internet then this will tell you where. Perfect for tracing stolen photographs, especially those of celebrities and models.

-Never send money, no matter how little or how much they try to persuade you.

-Ask a friend for their opinion. They will often see things that you are blind to.

-Don't go to them – get them to come and meet you at their own expense. It goes without saying that you should meet in a public place and never give them your home address.

-Look out for inconsistencies. If something doesn't sound right it probably isn't. Don't be afraid to question them on it. If they are genuine there's no need to get defensive when asked.

-Check their spelling and grammar. As they are usually based overseas, English won't be their first language and they'll make lots of strange mistakes.

-Don't fool yourself. Ask yourself why they'd really be interested in you, especially if there is a wide age gap or a big distance.

Check out the Scammer Databases on the Internet. You can read stories about all the people who have been duped so you can avoid the same fate. You'll be able to search for email addresses, photographs and names to see if any warning signals come up. I've included a few of the main ones at the end of this book.

Finally, there's no point trying to confront them and let them know you are on to them. All they will do is deny it and they'll use any information you give them to improve their scamming skills for the next person. Remember, these are nasty criminal gangs so you don't want to start antagonising them.

What to Do About Them

These people are evil and must be stopped. If you have suspicions that someone isn't who they appear to be, then cut off all contact immediately. Block their profile on the site and don't message them again. Don't delete any emails you've had from them as you may need them as evidence one day.

If you have already given them your email address or phone number then block them there too. You can usually do this by checking your email settings and calling your phone network provider.

If you do happen to have a bad experience then always report it to the site and go to the police if necessary. Don't be embarrassed or blame yourself. It's only by doing something about them that they'll be caught. If you won't do it for yourself, do it to stop them ruining the lives of the other singles out there.

Again, I do want to stress that dating sites (at least the paid ones) do get rid of virtually all the scammers. They are pretty good at it and you don't need to worry about them too much. You are more likely to get conned while you are out and about.

Protecting yourself is all about using your common sense. Ask yourself what their true motives might be and if something or someone seems too good to be true then they might well be.

Chapter Ten : How to get Unlimited Dates through Social Media Sites

Do you know what THE biggest dating sites in the world are right now? It's not Match.com, POF.com or Eharmony....it's Facebook. In fact, 40% of online daters are also proactively seeking dates through social media.

It's not too hard to work out why this is. They are completely free, almost everyone is on there and they are used throughout the world. They aren't officially dating sites but if you know what you are doing you can use them very effectively. In fact, the technology is so good on Facebook that many official dating companies use this to power their own sites. Quite a few even allow you to log in using your Facebook details to save time.

Using social media sites like Facebook, Twitter and LinkedIn for dating is not a new thing. Some people have been using them for years for this very purpose. They have huge, active databases that you can effortlessly search on and almost everyone has a profile photo. What's not to love?

The sad truth is that getting a date on any social media site is not as easy as it may sound and many people are terrible at it. You get the same issues as paid online dating sites. It tends to be men who contact women on these sites, inundating them with friend requests, cheesy pickup lines or gushing compliments. While every girl adores compliments, coming across as desperate is never going to win them over.

Don't worry, I'm going to show you how you can find your hot date through the use of your social media accounts. It absolutely can be done and I know that because I met my wife on Myspace which was once the Social Media King.

The Basics of Social Media and Getting a Date

Almost everyone is on one form of social media site or another. With less time for an active social life, people turn to social media to stay connected to the world as well as their friends and family. This trend will only grow as time goes on. It's a perfect blend of distraction, time wasting and fun.

So one day you are sitting at your desk, a little bored and start scanning through random websites, when you decide to visit your friend's profile. Suddenly you are stuck on a pretty/handsome face smiling at you from a display picture. You have learned their name and basic information, so you can move on to the next step. Some obviously single people on these sites can get many friend requests (or followers) each week which they prefer to ignore. This means there is a good chance of you being placed into the black hole of requests or never seen at all.

You've got to stand out if you want to make this work. The same rules of online dating apply for your social media profile. Make sure that you have an attention grabbing profile and use your best photo on the page. If you are on a site that has your photo album, make sure that only the good ones are visible to "the public." Oh and the same goes for your updates too. You don't want to scare off a potential date with strange photos or have them knowing your every move. Always set your privacy settings so that strangers can only see the best side of what you get up to.

Fun and Flirting on Facebook

Facebook is now the number one social media site and will therefore naturally have the biggest pool of singles. The problem is that they aren't as easy to reach as they once were due to site policy changes.

When Facebook first launched it was possible to run a search to find other singles who lived in your area and then message them immediately. However, this feature was removed once they realized they could make much more money promoting other online dating companies. This resulted in endless adverts to "Meet Hot Girls in your Area" or visit the "Site where all the Singles Are" from third parties. Lots of money was spent by all the white label dating companies too, paying good money to compete for your attention. The end result was that dating adverts were about the most complained about adverts due to them being so oversaturated. This resulted in Facebook placing a complete ban on the smaller companies advertising at all. It's now only the big boys – the market leaders in the dating world – that are allowed to advertise.

I predict that one day, when users get tired of these adverts too, then Facebook will evolve once again. Gone will be the adverts and instead a paid dating feature will come in. You'll be able to pay to search for other singles that live in your area and contact them immediately. Sound familiar? If you think they will never charge, then think again. They already do make you pay if you want to send a message to a person that you have no mutual friends with. This ranges from a tiny amount to a much larger one if you want to try your luck with celebrities.

The good news for you is that for now the singles are still on there and contactable....you just have to do it the right way.

First and foremost, do not send someone you like a friend request straightaway. The chances of getting blocked and being marked as a spam is extremely high. If this happens too many times then you run the risk of getting your account permanently deleted. You have to make an effort and use all your charm to woo that special one. It's still a lot easier than actually going out in public to meet someone and completely free too.

Do not try posting an impulsive message on their wall directly either, even if their privacy settings allow it. You'll get overlooked as they won't have a clue who you are. It doesn't look mysterious and exciting, it looks cheap and desperate.

So what exactly are you supposed to do? Well there are two scenarios when it comes to strangers (or even with people that you haven't spoken to much in a long time).

Check to see if you both might have any friends in common. If you do have mutual friends, you have the freedom to use the power of the Facebook POKE.

Once you've done this, your target will be notified you poked them the next time they log in. Now here comes the most crucial part. If you are lucky enough to get a poke back then you know that they have gone through your profile and must have found you interesting. At this point, you may have to take your chances. When this Poke and getting Poked activity has been done 2-3 times, it's time to drop them a message.

Make sure you start by striking up an interesting conversation. You have to be witty and thoughtful if you want to make a memorable first impression. How you do this varies on individual style. Coming across as aggressive and dull is a big turn off for most people. You can always try *"Hey poke buddy, how are you?"* or if you have known the person for years, you could easily write *"It's been a long time, how are you?"* If he/she is not within your network, you have to take your chances by simply dropping them a message, without trying to come across as a desperate stalker. If you choose this route do not use lines like, *"Can I be your friend"* or *"Do you want to have a poke with me in real life".* These lines are out of date and make you seem boring. You are going to have to stand out so be humorous, decent and interesting enough for him/her to reply and stay engaged in the conversation.

Did you get a reply back from them? If you did then they clearly like you and you can carry on talking. If you didn't then try once again using a different tactic. If there is no message after that then you need to be smart and move on to the next attractive profile. Talking about common interests is strongly advisable and is sure to be a safe topic to start with. It makes you appear more open towards the other person and is the best way to show you would get on in the real world. Nothing opens up people more than talking about what they love to do for fun and their interests. Then ask them a question about something topical or about their friends and family.

Remember to be a good listener, otherwise you will end up labelled as selfish. The key to building any good foundation is just by having a good conversation. By actively listening and engaging in good conversation striking a date on any social media site will be so much easier for you. Now that you have the attention and full interest of the person, next step is to talk about personal lives. Once you reach this level, it is better to carry out conversations through text message or phone calls. If you follow my recommended techniques then there should be no major issues into finding a date through social media.

Using your Existing Friends and Networks to Help

There's a much better way of getting dates from Social Media sites and that's by using your existing social circle. You probably have hundreds of friends who you can ask to act as your own matchmaker.

Make your friend feel special and that you respect their opinion. You do this by messaging them personally telling them that you are looking for love and need their help. If you send everyone a message in a group email format you'll never get a reply.

You could spend time scanning through their own friend lists seeing who you might be attracted to and ask for an introduction. This isn't a great idea as your friend will have to contact them all individually as and when you let them know. If it requires too much effort then they probably won't be bothered. A better strategy would be to ask if they know anyone suitable. They will have a fair and much more realistic idea about who you might be a suitable match for.

If you are feeling brave, ask them to write a post on their Facebook walls announcing they are helping you by playing Cupid. They should include your photograph and a few lines about you. If they have anyone interested they can connect you.

It's probably not wise to ask an ex-partner to help you find a new one, unless you are still very close. Even if they have good intentions, their friends will probably find it all a bit weird and be wary of dating you.

There are hundreds, if not thousands of dating related pages and groups on Facebook. This can be a good place to find singles but it's also where Scammers hang out. This won't be a problem for you as you'll have read my chapter on how to spot them. If you've jumped ahead, then I do advise you to take a look. After all, these conmen won't just target you on dating sites but via your email account. Spam messages flood our inboxes every single day.

Twitter Tactics

Using Twitter to get a date is much easier than you probably imagined. Everyone writes in short messages of 140 characters or less so you won't have to spend too long thinking about what to say. You can see what they look like and most have visible profiles. It's not a dating site, so if you are primarily using the site for this purpose then you need to be a little sneaky. This is what you need to do:

If anyone wants to be successful at using Twitter, they have to keep on top of things and monitor the site regularly. If they write a message there is only a very limited time frame for their followers to see it. Keep an eye on who has posted recently, within the last few minutes. More likely than not, they'll still be online keeping an eye to see if anyone comments on what they've written. If you target these then you'll have a good chance of getting a reply.

As with all these sites, you'll obviously have a wonderful profile photo and an interesting, attention getting introduction.

If someone takes a look at who you are following or what you've been tweeting to people, then you are going to be rumbled pretty quickly. To avoid this, follow people of both sexes so your following statistics look about average. If you are a guy looking for girls and you are only following hot girls then your plan will be really obvious. The same goes for everything you post.

Talk about how exciting your life is and ask people dating questions. Retweet or Favourite the posts of the people you would like to know better. They'll be notified and it draws back the attention to you. Every now and again it's worth being blatant and posting something obvious about you being actively single.

LinkedIN to Love

LinkedIN is purely about business so you should never use it for dating. At least that's what you are supposed to think. Believe it or not, LinkedIn is not just a great social networking platform for people looking for jobs. You don't have to be a Personnel or Human Resources specialist to find LinkedIn exciting. In fact, if you are looking for a date, you can use LinkedIn. Seriously. You just need to be extra careful and use it wisely, keeping under the radar as with Twitter.

There's only a very limited amount of information available on each profile. You can't find out if they are single or how they are, but simply where they are based and where they work. You only have one profile photo to decide if you find them attractive or not. So why is it so good? The fact that most people don't consciously use LinkedIn as a dating site gives you a tremendous competitive advantage. While it has the structural elements of a dating site - interest search and detailed profiles - most LinkedIn users are focused on the non-dating uses of the site. This leaves a lot of its treasure trove of singles for you.

LinkedIN does have an advantage over other social media sites when it comes to dating. This is the very useful "who viewed your profile" feature. This a great research tool if you want to find out who is paying closer attention to you than others. If you aren't a full member then you are limited to only seeing the last three, but if you log in regularly then this won't matter.

I'd never advise you to contact someone on the site, blindly asking if they are single. You'll be blocked, reported and removed in the time it takes you to make a cup of coffee. You'll do much better if you follow my special plan:

Work out what you are Interested in

LinkedIn lets people network, based on their shared interests. Usually, this is business or job-related. However, you can attract the attention of members of the opposite sex by emphasizing the interests you're most passionate about. While your profile should still retain the overall appearance of a LinkedIn professional profile, there should be enough information in your profile that should grab the eyes of someone of the opposite sex who shares those interests and passions.

Once you've figured out what these are, make sure you create a LinkedIn profile that highlights your passions. You shouldn't just list them out but describe them in a fun, attention-grabbing way. Keep in mind that just because you wrote your profile this way doesn't mean you'll automatically gain the attention of people you want to reach, you have to do several other steps.

Join Groups on LinkedIn and Engage in Community Discussions

Next, join groups on LinkedIn where people interested in the stuff you're passionate about would hang out at. This shouldn't be too difficult since LinkedIn has tons of communities. It seems that they have a group for whatever interest people can come up with. These groups are like mini conversation forums. There are quite a few on there just for singles such as the "Single Professionals Network (SPIN)" Once you eliminate the dating companies and coaches (like me) giving dating advice, you'll find plenty of possible targets. After this, try some groups based on your hobbies and general activities.

After joining, engage in community discussions. Don't be a wallflower. Stand out by participating. This doesn't mean being an attention hog but by helping others and enjoying what they have to say.

Draw Attention to Yourself by Sharing Compelling Content

There is a wrong way and a right way of bringing attention to yourself in Linkedin groups. The best way is to stay on topic and share only the very best and most compelling content that is directly relevant to the subject of the groups you are a member of.

These can be from websites, news sites, or blogs, or some other sources. Always add some commentary or at least a comment with your shared content links.

Eventually, people would be drawn to you because you share the best stuff or you are highly engaged in the group.

Engage Group Members of the Opposite Sex

When you notice attractive members of the opposite sex, step up the engagement level and converse with them. At the very worst, you'll make a new friend. At best, they'll scope out your profile and see how much of a match you are and you two can go on to deeper levels of conversation. This will begin as connections, then you'll start communicating with each other through LinkedIn and then, if things pan out, through email or Skype.

Make no mistake about it, LinkedIn can be a great source of dates. You just have to structure and position your presence on this powerful social networking platform in such a way that you attract dates instead of investment or job opportunities.

Letting the World Know you Exist

There is one more, absolutely fantastic thing you can do if you want to get some SERIOUS interest with Social Media. I've had clients try it and get astounding results: Set up your own dating blog!

If you do this, it will stop you getting banned and give you a legitimate reason for using them for this purpose. You're treating it as your own little business so it's fine to promote it on Twitter, Linked IN and the like. It's so easy - you write a blog post and then share it on the various sites. This can even be done automatically every time you make it live.

It's very easy to create a blog. You can go to a site such as WordPress and have one up and running within five minutes. It's completely free and you can make it look how you want using a wide variety of templates. The title doesn't need to be too clever if you don't want it to be. "Emily's Dating Adventures" or "1001 Dates in Denver" are perfectly good. Use the blog to share your funny dating stories about your dates or to encourage discussion about interesting topics. There's a captive audience of single people out there who love checking out blogs to get dating advice or see what everyone else is up to.

There are lots of dating blogs out there now and these will only continue to grow. If you want to get traffic to your own you've got to be worth reading. You don't need to be the greatest writer on the planet, but you will have to have a story to tell. I know you've got stories in you so let them out and you'll get singles from all over the world wanting to join in.

Chapter Eleven : Love at First Swipe – Dating Apps and The Future of Dating

More people are logging in to online dating sites from their phones than through a computer than ever before. Dating is becoming much more mobile and as such, dating apps like Blendr, Tinder and Twine are becoming increasingly common. Blendr followed in the footsteps of Grindr, the gay dating app. Dating apps were originally used purely for casual hook ups and had a somewhat sleazy reputation. With these, singles can locate each other quickly in the same area and meet for the pure purpose of sex. Women in particular were reluctant to give this information as they were concerned about their safety.

The revolutionary new dating app Tinder may be the first to change opinion and is succeeding where so many others have failed. This is thanks to its flirty, fun design and the fact it only gives your rough location. It's been quickly followed by lots of other dating apps. The most interesting of these is Twine – where all the photos are blurred out – putting the focus on the actual profile.

A Quick Guide to Tinder

TINDER, is THE dating app of choice for many singles that are looking for fun, friends, and maybe even that special someone to love; almost everyone is on this very popular dating app. That's why this is the app I'm going to teach you how to use, above all others.

While the company has not made it public knowledge of the number of accounts that have been created since it launched , Tinder users have been busy rating each other's profile 3.5 billion times a day and have been lucky to have matched up 45 million singles according to Forbes Magazine.

How does this App work?

It is a ridiculously simple idea. Once you have downloaded the app onto your smartphone and set up your profile, you are ready to "Tinder", if you will. After your profile is created using your Facebook link, people will begin to be able to view your profile. You can then start viewing and liking other profiles that take your fancy. All you have to do is press the button to show your interest or swipe on the next one. If one of those people likes you too, Tinder will make the introduction and allow you to chat within the app.

The best thing about this is that there's no rejection. You have no idea how many profiles are active and you'll be swiping/liking so fast that you'll only care when you get a mutual match.

Before you Start Chatting

Much like any other app or website that allows you to create a profile and meet new people, you will want to adhere to and remember some guidelines that will help you to have a better experience.

Tinder will show a small sample of your Facebook profile text along with a few photos lifted straight from the site. This text is completely editable, so you should take the time to make sure it makes you sound amazing. The same rules for online dating apply here but most people don't bother. If you bother to craft it carefully then you'll be ahead of your competition. If you follow my tips then you'll be racking up dates in seconds.

Use a Tagline to your Benefit

As you set up your profile, you are given the option to enter in a tagline. This is a very short sentence summary that you can use to describe yourself or what you are looking for. This is your opportunity to show a little piece of yourself and to get some attention. So, be funny and say something that will get you noticed.

Do your Research

If you have any mutual friends in common on Facebook then this will be displayed on the screen. Contact them to find out more about the person you are getting to know. You can never have too much insider information. They might be able to alert you if someone isn't worth your time or effort, or perhaps they will give you some tips to attract them instead.

Make Good Banter

When you get a hit you have to be ready to back it up. It is really self-explanatory; be funny and quick in your replies, try to come up with something that is original and makes the person want to keep talking to you every time. It can go a long way and make a real difference in the long term.

Don't use your Profile for the Purpose of Promoting your Business

There is not one person you will find on any social media network that will want to hear a business pitch on how they can earn more money or generate more followers on other social media networks they are on. So just stick to dating unless you want your account removed.

Spelling and Grammar: Make Sure you Check them

Using words like 'your' instead of 'you're' or not using a comma will quickly get you blocked. By using proper grammar is always good and will quickly earn you the respect you want.

No Group Photos

Many people want to know and not assume which person you are; do not create confusion where confusion is not wanted. Have the confidence to show yourself as you are...do not hide "behind" a group.

Do not Post Topless Photos

It is great that you have the confidence to show off your boobs or the abs you've worked so hard on. BUT leave a little mystery to be discovered when the time is right. Taking that away before they ever have a chance to make the discovery for themselves is just a turn off.

No Explicit Messages

It comes off as just creepy; especially if it is the first message. If that is how you are going to start out, it is very likely that people will assume you are only going to get worse and do you really want to be that girl or guy?

Give a Person the Chance they deserve

It's very easy to become too fussy but this could lead to you running out of matches in your area. You may not be instantly attracted to them at first but still why not give them a chance. Often pictures do not give a person the justice they deserve and people will make the assumption that they are not as good as a person as their picture shows. Just give love a chance!

Meet them!

The biggest complaint I hear about apps like Tinder is that people aren't willing to meet. If you are just going to text back and forth then you're going to be single for a very long time. It can quickly become a time wasting distraction that will stop you meeting a real partner. The only success stories you'll hear are from those who bit the bullet and met face to face in the real world. Life is short so get out there and take a little risk.

It's not a Replacement for Online Dating

This can be a fantastic little ego boost. Every time you get a match you get a warm fuzzy feeling inside. Yes, someone likes me! The problem is that it tends to attract people who want to flirt and aren't necessarily looking for a long term relationship. You won't be able to find out much about them as the profile text is so short. Online dating is much better as you can find out all the little important details (such as height, hobbies etc) that help you find out if you are a match. Tinder is much more hit and miss.

With these helpful tips, you will not only have a profile people will be interested in but you will begin to meet many more people than you ever thought possible. You never really know who you will meet in this world and how they can change your life for the better. Take a chance!

How to Avoid Cheats and Timewasters on Dating Apps

Dating apps can be an easy, fast way to search for single people who happen to be in your area. You can log in from your mobile phone, add a photo and get up and running very quickly. However, because it's so simple it can be great tool for those already in relationships. It's a perfect tool for having an affair if they are of that mind-set. With no fees to pay or sites to log in to, there's no evidence trail for them to get caught out. Here is my advice on how to avoid these vile people:

Why are they never available? Married people or those in relationships tend to have a lot less free time alone than singles. So be wary if you find they are too busy to meet or chat with you at weekends or during the evening. If they are only communicating during the day then perhaps they can't use the app in front of their partner. This is a good reason why you should also talk to them on the phone before meeting.

Get a reference. One of the great features with Tinder is that you can see if you have any mutual friends on Facebook. So there's no harm in asking your friend to vouch for them. They may well have more of an idea about whether they are a trustworthy single or long term married with kids.

Study the photos. As the photos can be taken from Facebook their best shots may be from their wedding day. It's amazing how many married people use their wedding album shots as a Tinder image. They will of course deny it if you confront them and say they are now divorced or were just a wedding guest, so trust your instincts.

Remember your safety. Some apps will notify others to the rough locations you are at. Don't tell them exactly where you are or go to them. Instead, meet in another place that you know will be busy with lots of other people. That way you can get rid of them if you aren't comfortable they are telling you the truth.

It's still too easy to get a fake profile. Some people will create fake Facebook accounts or even set up a duplicate with their real photos and a different name. That way it will look legitimate although they can tell their other halves they had their identity stolen. If they look or seem too good to be true then they probably are. Ask yourself why a stunning supermodel would need or have time to be messing around with dating apps.

The vast majority of people who use these apps have no intention of ever meeting up. Instead, it's useful as a quick ego boost or fun flirt when you are bored. I believe this will change over time as more people get used to how they work and more women start to use them. In the meantime, if you are looking for a long term relationship then you are better off sticking to regular dating sites. Many have their own app version anyway which you can download once you become a member.

The Future of Online Dating

According to Online Dating Magazine, 99% of new online dating start-ups fail to ever make a profit. Dating is seen as an easy way to make money as everyone has a desire to fall in love. There's now too much competition all aiming for exactly the same customers.

Does that mean that the online dating bubble has burst? Absolutely not!

The existing companies are having to work harder to keep members interested. This can only lead to innovation and an overall better user experience.

Changes are happening in the dating industry all the time though. One of the most important of these is that Online Dating sites are slowly killing off speed dating and paid singles parties. That's because many are now running their own free dating events as an added bonus for their members. It's a worrying trend that has seen many bigger players go under and they couldn't compete.

While free might seem better, it actually greatly reduces the quality of the events. There is no longer any money available to pay for staff to run activities, look after guests and introduce them to each other. There is no budget for entertainment or customer support afterwards. The events offer little more than getting single people together in a bar and leaving them to their own devices. This ignores the fact that it was their reluctance to do this that attracted them to online dating in the first place. It may initially sound good but most people are shy and need help to interact.

Singles will tire of free events and become prepared once again to pay for a ticket. New themes, concepts and ideas will be needed in order to attract them.

What will Happen Next?

Dating apps will eventually become more popular than dating sites. Your phone is always next to you at the times it's impossible to access a computer. You can chat away while you're on the train, at work, watching the television or even in the bath (if you're careful.)   At the moment these apps are a novelty and don't cost anything. This lowers the overall quality and they are plagued with timewasters and fake profiles. This is frustrating as the apps themselves are great fun and easy to use. I firmly believe that professionals will be prepared to pay for a dating app that has quality singles on it. The best online dating sites will be the ones who also run the best dating apps. The easier the apps are to use then the more likely people will want to use them.

When it comes to online dating we've only seen the very tip of the iceberg in terms of what is possible. Over the next few years, technology will improve even more and with it will come new ideas and new possibilities. Only the very best last the distance but the overall winners are going to be all the singles. The opportunities to meet each other are only going to improve and the future of dating is very exciting indeed.

I can't wait to see what comes along, so I can keep up to date and continue to teach everyone how to be successful. You can find out all the latest dating trends, insights and innovations by reading the blog on my website.

Chapter Twelve : Happily Ever After: (How to Keep it Going)

I was very tempted to call this chapter "Keeping it Up!" but I think I'll save that for my next book title instead.

My wish for you is that you find that one special amazing person that you will spend the rest of your life with. I can't tell you how long this journey will take, but hopefully I've taught you everything you need to know to shorten the process. You may date lots of different people or it may take just a few. Either way, not all of these will work out… and that's absolutely fine. With each person you'll have new experiences and learn a little more about yourself. Eventually, before you know it – BANG – you've found them, are looking for sofas together and you're officially a couple.

In this last chapter I want to show you what to do once you start "seeing" someone and how to avoid the common errors people make that can destroy relationships.

How Soon Should I Commit?

Everyone longs for some form of connection with someone else. Beginning a relationship can be a difficult new step in someone's life. Rushing into a relationship is bound to cause issues at one point or another. Going too slow could also give mixed messages to the receiving end. It can never be perfectly clear as to how soon a relationship should become serious. This may be different for everyone, but in general the same guidelines can be followed.

New Beginnings

In the start of a relationship, it is important to keep things slow. As much as you may want to steadily move along, this will not benefit either of you. If you are dating someone who pressures you to advance, they may not be the right one for you. When starting down a new path, it is easy to find yourself confused. This can lead to the horrible mistake of following the crowd. Just because others around you may be rushing or diving headfirst into relationships doesn't mean you should do the same. Get to know the person you are dating by having deep involved and regular conversations.

What to Do

Before committing yourself to this person, take them out on a couple of dates. A simple dinner and/or movie will suffice. Do not do anything too fancy or overly romantic. This could scare your interest away. In most cases it is best to not be too serious, even if that is what you long to do. Trying to be serious in the start can come across as desperate. Be friendly, conversational and remain interested throughout the entire relationship.

When to Commit

If the courtship has gone well, it may be time to take the next step. By this point you should be able to read this person reasonably well. If being together still seems awkward and tense, this is definitely not the time to move forward. Ease further into the relationship. After a few dates, propose going steady. Making the relationship official is subtle, but a nice small step toward commitment. Your date can end up being disinterested or nervous about continuing on. After some time if they decide they are not interested, respect their wishes. On the other hand, if they seem nervous, reassure them that you understand and are willing to take things slowly. The right time will come to take that next step. If online dating is the case, it is up to you to figure if meeting in person is the right choice.

Don't Ruin Everything

More times than not, relationships have been destroyed by a rushed relationship. Generally, one partner may feel overwhelmed or even pressured. This can especially occur if you've had sex! Unless two people are already in a serious and very committed relationship, it is in everyone's best interest to not engage in sexual activity too quickly. Not only can this end a relationship, but it may cause extreme discomfort that did not need to happen. Before advancing on to such a strong point, be sure both of you are ready. Online dating does not usually last very long before you start taking things into the real world.

Building up to a strong and steady relationship can take months. Sometimes couples seem to be very serious from the very start. Keep things moderately slow to ensure both partners are on the same page. In some cases, a very serious relationship can take almost a year. A relationship should be enjoyed and savoured.

So take all the time you need. If you want to commit after two dates, two months or two years then it's completely your choice. Just make sure you are both happy and having fun!

When you are in a relationship then neither of you can ever afford to stop putting the effort in. If you ever do that and find yourselves stuck in a rut doing the same things, talk about it and spice things up. Let them know how much you love them as often as you can.

Are they Really the Right Person for You?

Please don't jump into a bad relationship just because it's easier than being on your own. If you've been single for a while then it might be tempting to think that this is the best you deserve, even if you are unhappy. That really is complete nonsense.

If you want a longer term future then you must question whether they are really marriage material. You've got the rest of your life to look forward to so be absolutely sure that you are with the right person to spend it with.

How do they make your feel? If they make your life that little bit better and you are able to share your secrets, dreams and love with each other, then they are the one. If they constantly ridicule, annoy or moan at you then this is a toxic relationship.

Sometimes letting go is the best option, as painful as it may feel at the time. Spend some time alone and then get yourself back out there in the dating world again. There is someone perfect for you, just waiting to meet you.

Dealing with Jealousy and Trust Issues in a Relationship

Strong relationships are stable, easy going, and loving. But, humans tend to succumb to human nature, which means that certain feelings and expectations can cause things to come crashing down. The prime cause of harm to a relationship is distrust. In many cases, there will be a party in a relationship that is distrusting, suspicious, and extremely jealous. While many couples allow jealousy to affect the relationship in a negative manner, there are ways to keep things stable and to avoid destruction. Here are some great ways in which you can keep your relationship safe and stable by coping with jealousy and distrust.

Cost Benefit Analysis

While this section may seem quite formal, it really isn't as technical as the title suggests. When it comes to a jealous relationship, you certainly want to do a cost-benefit analysis. If you find yourself exerting more energy, time, and negative feelings compared to the benefits of love and care, then you want to try to salvage what there is left of your relationship or move on. At the end of the day, if you aren't as happy as you should be, then assessing the relationship and making a decision is the best way to resolve the problem.

Talk With Your Significant Other

Perseverance is extremely important in a relationship, and if you are to overcome jealous and trust problems, then you need to have a serious talk with your partner. Without discussion of the issue, there will not be resolution. If your partner is the jealous one, sit them down and talk with them. Try to get to the root of the problem about why they are jealous, why they mistrust you, and what you can do to prevent these feelings from occurring. Another key point in this step is to make it clear that trust is the foundation of a relationship, and if your significant other cannot trust you, then the relationship itself will not be able to succeed.

Help a Partner Feel Safe

Jealousy and trust problems usually stem from insecurity or painful experiences in the past that has caused such feelings. If the problems arise from insecurity, then you need to find out from your partner what you can do to help them feel more secure. Quite often security can be developed by being around more often, showing dedication, and being affectionate towards your significant other. On the other hand, if the trust problems and jealousy arise from past history, then you need to set down some important points. First, make it clear that you aren't your partner's past flame. Next, you should also point out that just because a past partner made mistakes, it does not mean that you will do the same. Making these things clear can ease your significant other's feelings and can also help create a more positive and loving relationship.

Overall, trust problems are a big issue to deal with. But if you can go through the above recommendations, you may just be able to prevent the jealousy from overtaking your relationship. When you overcome issues like these then it can really strengthen your bond.

The Right Time to Delete your Profile

There's only one time when you should delete your profile: If you end up in a long term relationship. You don't want someone stumbling upon it and asking strange questions years later. If you are happy and settled then please don't keep your profile open. It's unfair to anyone who looks at it, as you will never respond. I also don't want you dipping back in for a quick ego boost to see if anyone likes you either. It's tempting to do that sometimes but you can't if it's not there. Do the deletion together while you remove both profiles and do it as a celebration and sign of a commitment to each other.

Never delete your profile in a fit of annoyance or because you aren't getting any interest. It won't cost you anything to keep it active, even if you aren't a subscriber. Leave it there while you are single as you don't know who may contact you tomorrow. Trust me, you never know when it's your time to suddenly get lucky. If ever you are unsure, wait 24 hours and then think about whether you want to pack everything in. You don't want to miss out on opportunities due to a little temporary frustration.

The same applies when you've started seeing someone and it's very early days. It can be tempting to stop using the site as it won't feel right to keep using it. That's fair enough, but again you shouldn't delete your account until you are absolutely ready. If you do and things don't work out for whatever reason, it can be frustrating having to start all over again.

When the time does come that you've met someone and you are both absolutely ready to delete your accounts, don't do it immediately. Consider taking a screenshot of your profiles and saving some of the messages you sent each other back at the beginning. Once you've deleted it then it's gone forever and you'll have lost the chance to look back on how you met. Dating sites shouldn't keep records of profiles/messages due to data protection laws so it's up to you if you want to make copies before you start your life together.

PLEASE: I strongly request that you always drop the website a quick thank you email as they rely on success stories to grow their businesses. You don't need to give your real names or provide photos unless you want to. If you do, you may find you might get a bottle of champagne or some other lovely surprise. The majority of people forget to do this which is a real shame. Don't be embarrassed but be proud of your achievement instead. If something works then you should give them the credit!

Meeting and Getting on with their Friends and Family

There comes a time at the start of every new relationship, where you have to do something that often seems very scary. You've been seeing each other for a little while and all is going well. Then suddenly, out of the blue it hits you. You knew it was coming but weren't prepared for it to happen so soon.

It's time to meet the family!

This is an experience that can really make you sweat. I've been there. Rather than see this as a really positive move, you think more and more about all the things that might go wrong. What if they don't like you? What if YOU can't stand them? What if you fancy his brother? What if you kill their cat in some bizarre door-shutting accident? These kinds of thoughts can keep you awake at night. Maybe it's better just to call the whole thing off and avoid the agony! I'm here to help you face this as confidently, and in a stress-free way, as possible.

It's a key moment in every long term relationship but it really doesn't have to be traumatic. Here are some tips I've put together to help you get through this experience:

Relax - It's very likely that they'll be nervous about meeting you too. They also want to make a good impression! The last thing they want is to embarrass themselves.

Treat it like another date - You need to present a positive image of yourself, so dress well and make sure you are well groomed.

Bring a Gift - Whatever you do, don't turn up empty handed. If it's a dinner party, bring some wine. If it's a birthday get a small gift. Mums always love flowers and they'll never forget you made the effort.

Do your Research - Find out who exactly you'll be meeting and work out some talking points in advance. Try and see if you have any mutual interests, such as sports, television or hobbies. It's much easier to keep the conversation flowing if you have already planned lots to chat about.

Smile - Everyone else will know each other, so they will already have their own inside jokes, memories and stories. You won't follow everything that gets said so just keep smiling and don't look bored! As long as you look like you are having fun and enjoying yourself then everyone else will be able to relax, allowing you to bond faster.

Avoid controversial remarks or jokes - especially when you are meeting elderly relatives.

Online Dating - Agree in advance about whether you're going to tell the truth about how and where you met. The taboo of meeting online has long gone, and I'd suggest you are always honest with your nearest and dearest, but if you aren't comfortable, just pretend your first date was also your first meeting. As long as you both stick to your story it will probably never need to be mentioned again.

How to Survive a Long Distance Relationship

Sometimes you might end up dating people who don't live near you. It's so easy to meet people from all over the world using the internet that this can be 8 miles or 800 miles. These relationships can be hard to keep going but they really can work if you are both prepared

Here is what you should do to keep the spark:

1) Communicate often. Make sure you talk as often as you can and send regular emails and texts. Talking on the phone is vital as you need to be able to hear their voice. Without hearing them speak, it's very hard to work on any form of romantic connection.

2) Try and see each other as often as you can, even if it means sacrificing things. The times you do spend together will be all the more powerful.

3) A long distance relationship is built on one thing – Trust. You don't want to have to be worrying about what the other person might be getting up to.

4) The same rules for dating apply even if you aren't seeing each other as much. You are still together so don't be needy, demanding or controlling or you will quickly destroy everything.

5) What's the long term plan? Will one of you eventually move near the other? If neither of you has any intention of relocating then the relationship could be doomed from the start. Set a time limit when you agree to discuss it again and to see if anything has changed.

6) Do something at the same time, like watching a film or reading the same book. You can talk about it afterwards and it will be as if you are together.

7) Use Skype – the most loved tool for long distance lovers. Free calls over the internet and you'll be able to see each other on webcam too.

8) Give them a personal object of yours so in a time of need, when they miss you, they are able to hold on to something that once belonged to you.

Don't Give Up

Many people seem to give up far too easily and quickly when it comes to dating. Perhaps they will join a dating site, send out some messages and then get disappointed when they don't get many replies. Or maybe they'll attend a singles event and not find anyone they like there.

Rather than keep at it, they'll think "Oh, I've tried that and it didn't work. Now I can cross that off my list." I know that it can sometimes seem exhausting if you don't get instant results but dating is a trial and error process and the more you do, the better you'll get at it

Yes, you'll make mistakes at the start but please don't give up. Enjoy the fun and adventures you are having and all the new experiences you find coming your way.

You need to keep in mind that all my techniques really do work! Every day I hear success stories sent to me from people who struck lucky. The secret is to keep at it – like most things in life, you get out of it what you put into it. Otherwise it's like joining a gym, going twice and then quitting because you weren't miraculously fit and muscular. These things can take time.

One person said to me recently that they've calculated they would have to send out 100 messages to get 10 replies back which would lead to one or two dates. They just didn't have time to be sending out so many messages each week.

My reply to him was that he was thinking about the negative side of things rather than the reality. What if one of the first people he met up with turned out to be his Miss Right? He'd then be able to stop messaging people. Therefore, he should spend more time making sure he has the best profile, photos and messages possible right from the start. He can then be sure he's equipping himself with the best tools for the job. Anyway, if you are getting two dates a week from 100 short messages then something must be going right.

I can promise you that if you are proactive and positive you WILL find someone. You just need to turn off that annoying voice in your head that makes you think negative thoughts like "I will never meet anyone". Replace it with a louder, stronger voice telling you positive, encouraging statements like "I will meet someone very soon" and "They will be lucky to have me."

The more work you put in at the start, then the quicker you'll see the results. Online dating will take up a lot of your time, but there are plenty of other options too. Accept every invitation to go out that you get as you never know who might be there. If you aren't getting enough invitations then try speed dating or arranging your own dinner party.

If you ever find yourself tempted to give up try getting a friend to help you. Ask them to send out some messages with you or take a look at your profile. That way you'll get a whole new perspective on things and have support when you need it. If they are also single they can even go to some events with you.

It's very likely you might find yourself becoming TOO successful with online dating. It's not unusual to get a little overwhelmed with the sheer number of dates you are actually having. It can be difficult to find the energy and focus if this happens, so by all means have a dating holiday if necessary.

You can set aside two weeks where you promise yourself you won't even think about dating. This means no dates, no quick checks on messages and definitely no logging into Dating Apps. If you've been getting close to anyone, try and see them before your break or tell them you are going away – don't just leave them wondering where you've gone. Use the time to do all the things you've been neglecting. This could mean seeing your family or doing something nice for yourself. When the break is over, you'll feel renewed and excited about getting back to dating again. Sometimes a great new start means trying a completely new website. New members means new opportunities.

Oh and please have a life outside of dating. Don't let all your thoughts and actions be purely about your dating life. Keep yourself fit, healthy and active and never forget your family and friends need you.

I hope you've enjoyed this book as much as I've enjoyed writing it. It's taken me a long time to get it all together and I expect I'll have to regularly update it. That's the thing with the dating world, it's constantly evolving. You should be doing the same by getting new photos, changing sites and updating your profile every now and again.

I wish you every happiness and that you find the one you are looking for. If you ever need help then you know where to find me.

Until my next book, happy dating!

James

I WILL MAKE YOU CLICK

Dating Guru's Dating Directory

Online Dating Sites

As the internet continues to play a huge role in our lives, the number of online dating sites has skyrocketed. There are over 1,400 sites dedicated to dating in the UK alone, so it could be difficult finding out which one is the best fit for you. It's not possible to list them all here but the good ones are all on my website.

Here are the best of the best from around the world.

Match.com

Match.com is one of the most popular dating sites in the world with over a million members registered. Match boasts that their site has led to more successful relationships, dates and marriages than any other online dating company. With a large database full of many different kinds of people, it's almost guaranteed that you'll find someone interesting that you'd like to get to know more. You might have to sift through lots of profiles, but eventually odds are you'll find your match.

Plenty of Fish

Plenty of Fish is another huge dating site that offers both a free and paid membership option. POF.com has a huge member database with over 11 million members signed up so far. A unique feature on Plenty of Fish is that you can specify exactly what you are looking for with their site. You can look for friends, casual dating, long term dating and even marriage. This site is like a hybrid between a social network and a dating site where you can meet local singles or singles all over the world. Plenty of Fish has members in the UK, Canada, US, Australia, France, Ireland, Germany, New Zealand and Spain.

LoveStruck

One of my preferred UK dating sites is called LoveStruck.com. The premise of LoveStruck is letting people meet in large cities right away. If you're in London and you're free for lunch or dinner, LoveStruck allows you to search for their members by the nearest tube station. You can meet a date, have a bite to eat and then if you like each other keep in touch. It's great for on the go daters and those overwhelmed by meeting people in big cities.

Parship

Parship is another dating site that is a little different than some of the others. Parship is a site that finds matches for you based on a psychometric test you take after you set up your profile. It's a fun test with plenty of scientific study involved, and promises to set you up with people who are compatible for you. You'll have the chance to view your matches, chat with them online and if that goes well, set up a date in person.

Dating Vegetarian

If dating a fellow veggie lover is a must for you, you might want to check out datingvegetarian.co.uk. This site will let you search for fellow single vegetarians in your area.

Muddy Matches

Muddy Matches is a wonderful site for those who like a more country lifestyle. So if you love the countryside more than the towns this is probably the site for you. The team are very friendly and will do their best to help you on your dating journey.

AsianSingleSolution.com

If you are an Asian Indian professional then you must try out AsianSingleSolution.com. They have thousands of Hindu, Sikh and Muslim members and run regular singles parties to help you meet them.

Onlinedaterbase.com

Online Dater Base is home to one of the world's largest databases of singles. It's a very relaxed, fun site to use and I've heard some great successes from it. This is one of my own dating sites so I can definitely recommend it to you.

If you like specialty dating sites, you can also try JDate for finding Jewish singles, and Love Arts for those who are very fond of the arts

Other Useful Sites

Groupon

If you are doing a lot of dating you'll need to constantly think up fun new ideas. That's why deals sites such as Groupon are fantastic resources for scoping out offers and getting inspiration. One day they might have a discounted meal at a nearby restaurant, or another might be a wonderful Roller-skating Activity day. If you see something especially good, such as half price cocktails then you can usually buy more than one voucher.

YourTango

If you need some dating advice urgently then this is an incredibly useful site for you. It's full of expert blogs and help sections for every aspect of dating and relationships. Just run a search for a particular issue you might be having and you'll get an answer immediately.

Launching your Own Dating Site

If you are feeling ambitious or looking to grow your own brand, then why not start up your own dating site?

The best website for doing this is called Dating Factory. It's free to set up and they cover the hosting and design for you. All you need to do it come up with a clever name, put your unique spin on it and then promote it.

www.datingfactory.com

Scammer Databases

If you'd like to do a little research to find out if your prospective date is real, check out these websites:

http://scamdigger.com/

http://www.scammerlist.com/

http://www.romancescam.com/

Reverse Image Checking Sites
Google

http://www.google.com/insidesearch/features/images/searchbyimage.html

TinEye

https://www.tineye.com/

Personal Dating Coaching

If you are interested in having a professional Dating Coach work with you to help you with every aspect of dating there is only one option. That's to hire me! I work with clients from all over the world

www.jamespreece.com

Dating Apps

New dating apps pop up every day, but there are just three that I would suggest you use right now. These are the biggest three in the world so have the most members and useful features. They are all available through your mobile phone, so just have a look in your online store. This will depend on the make and model of your phone.

Tinder

Tinder is a matchmaking dating app which uses GPS to find you matches who are local to where you are based.

Zoosk

Zoosk has a unique Behavioural MatchmakingTM engine which learns as you click to match you with singles you're likely to be mutually attracted to.

Loveoo

Loveoo has a very smooth interface which makes it one of the most easy to use dating apps in the world.

About the Author

James Preece is the Dating Guru.

As the UK's leading Dating Expert and Dating Coach he is a consultant for many dating sites and is involved in a wide variety of different areas, such as personal dating coaching, Online Dating, speed dating and matchmaking.

He is a very experienced Relationship expert and is a rising star having already helped thousands of men and women find love, build confidence and improve their relationships.

He is a regularly featured expert in top UK and international media: such as the Independent, Cosmopolitan, FHM, Men's Health, Match.com, The Sun and Ann Summers amongst many more. He also runs very successful dating events both in the UK and is a regular consultant for many dating companies.

He has advised for various television and radio shows including the Online Dating episode of "You've Been Scammed" for BBC One.

For more information or to get in touch please visit his website:

www.jamespreece.com

Printed in Great Britain
by Amazon